THE
CIRCULATORY
SYSTEM

THE ENCYCLOPEDIA OF
HEALTH

THE HEALTHY BODY

Dale C. Garell, M.D. · General Editor

THE
CIRCULATORY
SYSTEM

Regina Avraham

Introduction by C. Everett Koop, M.D., Sc.D.
Surgeon General, U.S. Public Health Service

CHELSEA HOUSE PUBLISHERS
New York   Philadelphia

The goal of the ENCYCLOPEDIA OF HEALTH *is to provide general information in the ever-changing areas of physiology, psychology, and related medical issues. The titles in this series are not intended to take the place of the professional advice of a physician or other health-care professional.*

ON THE COVER: Engravings by Vesalius

Chelsea House Publishers
EDITOR-IN-CHIEF: Nancy Toff
EXECUTIVE EDITOR: Remmel T. Nunn
MANAGING EDITOR: Karyn Gullen Browne
COPY CHIEF: Juliann Barbato
PICTURE EDITOR: Adrian G. Allen
ART DIRECTOR: Maria Epes
MANUFACTURING MANAGER: Gerald Levine

The Encyclopedia of Health
SENIOR EDITOR: Jane Larkin Crain

Staff for THE CIRCULATORY SYSTEM
ASSOCIATE EDITOR: Paula Edelson
COPY EDITOR: Terrance Dolan
DEPUTY COPY CHIEF: Ellen Scordato
EDITORIAL ASSISTANT: Jennifer Trachtenberg
PICTURE RESEARCHER: Karen Herman
DESIGN: Debbie Jay, Jean Weiss
DESIGNER: Victoria Tomaselli
ASSISTANT DESIGNER: Marjorie Zaum
PRODUCTION COORDINATOR: Joseph Romano

3 5 7 9 8 6 4 2

Library of Congress Cataloging in Publication Data

Avraham, Regina.
  THE CIRCULATORY SYSTEM / Regina Avraham.
    p.   cm.—(The Encyclopedia of health)
  Bibliography: p.
  Includes index.
  Summary: Describes the organs of the circulatory system and their function. Also discusses heart problems and how they may be avoided.
  ISBN 0-7910-0013-3
        0-7910-0453-8 (pbk.)
  1. Cardiovascular system—Juvenile literature.   [1. Circulatory system.]   I. Title.   II. Series.   88-20260
  QP103.A94 1989   CIP
  612.1—dc 19   AC

CONTENTS

Prevention and Education: The Keys to Good Health—
C. Everett Koop, M.D., Sc.D.   7

Foreword—Dale C. Garell, M.D.   9

1 To a Long and Healthy Life   13

2 The History of Heart Study   17

3 Understanding the Heart and Blood Vessels   31

4 Understanding the Blood   43

5 Common Heart Problems   59

6 Treating Heart Problems   71

7 Preventing Heart Disease   85

Appendix: For More Information   97

Further Reading   99

Glossary   101

Index   105

THE ENCYCLOPEDIA OF
H E A L T H

THE HEALTHY BODY

The Circulatory System
Dental Health
The Digestive System
The Endocrine System
Exercise
Genetics & Heredity
The Human Body: An Overview
Hygiene
The Immune System
Memory & Learning
The Musculoskeletal System
The Neurological System
Nutrition
The Reproductive System
The Respiratory System
The Senses
Speech & Hearing
Sports Medicine
Vision
Vitamins & Minerals

THE LIFE CYCLE

Adolescence
Adulthood
Aging
Childhood
Death & Dying
The Family
Friendship & Love
Pregnancy & Birth

MEDICAL ISSUES

Careers in Health Care
Environmental Health
Folk Medicine
Health Care Delivery
Holistic Medicine
Medical Ethics
Medical Fakes & Frauds
Medical Technology
Medicine & the Law
Occupational Health
Public Health

PSYCHOLOGICAL DISORDERS
AND THEIR TREATMENT

Anxiety & Phobias
Child Abuse
Compulsive Behavior
Delinquency & Criminal Behavior
Depression
Diagnosing & Treating Mental Illness
Eating Habits & Disorders
Learning Disabilities
Mental Retardation
Personality Disorders
Schizophrenia
Stress Management
Suicide

MEDICAL DISORDERS
AND THEIR TREATMENT

AIDS
Allergies
Alzheimer's Disease
Arthritis
Birth Defects
Cancer
The Common Cold
Diabetes
Drugs: Prescription & OTC
First Aid & Emergency Medicine
Gynecological Disorders
Headaches
The Hospital
Kidney Disorders
Medical Diagnosis
The Mind-Body Connection
Mononucleosis & Other Infectious Diseases
Nuclear Medicine
Organ Transplants
Pain
Physical Handicaps
Poisons & Toxins
Sexually Transmitted Diseases
Skin Diseases
Stroke & Heart Disease
Substance Abuse
Tropical Medicine

PREVENTION AND EDUCATION: THE KEYS TO GOOD HEALTH

C. Everett Koop, M.D., Sc.D.
Surgeon General,
U.S. Public Health Service

The issue of health education has received particular attention in recent years because of the presence of AIDS in the news. But our response to this particular tragedy points up a number of broader issues that doctors, public health officials, educators, and the public face. In particular, it points up the necessity for sound health education for citizens of all ages.

Over the past 25 years this country has been able to bring about dramatic declines in the death rates for heart disease, stroke, accidents, and, for people under the age of 45, cancer. Today, Americans generally eat better and take better care of themselves than ever before. Thus, with the help of modern science and technology, they have a better chance of surviving serious—even catastrophic—illnesses. That's the good news.

But, like every phonograph record, there's a flip side, and one with special significance for young adults. According to a report issued in 1979 by Dr. Julius Richmond, my predecessor as Surgeon General, Americans aged 15 to 24 had a higher death rate in 1979 than they did 20 years earlier. The causes: violent death and injury, alcohol and drug abuse, unwanted pregnancies, and sexually transmitted diseases. Adolescents are particularly vulnerable, because they are beginning to explore their own sexuality and perhaps to experiment with drugs. The need for educating young people is critical, and the price of neglect is high.

Yet even for the population as a whole, our health is still far from what it could be. Why? A 1974 Canadian government report attrib-

7

uted all death and disease to four broad elements: inadequacies in the health-care system, behavioral factors or unhealthy life-styles, environmental hazards, and human biological factors.

To be sure, there are diseases that are still beyond the control of even our advanced medical knowledge and techniques. And despite yearnings that are as old as the human race itself, there is no "fountain of youth" to ward off aging and death. Still, there is a solution to many of the problems that undermine sound health. In a word, that solution is prevention. Prevention, which includes health promotion and education, saves lives, improves the quality of life, and, in the long run, saves money.

In the United States, organized public health activities and preventive medicine have a long history. Important milestones include the improvement of sanitary procedures and the development of pasteurized milk in the late 19th century, and the introduction in the mid-20th century of effective vaccines against polio, measles, German measles, mumps, and other once-rampant diseases. Internationally, organized public health efforts began on a wide-scale basis with the International Sanitary Conference of 1851, to which 12 nations sent representatives. The World Health Organization, founded in 1948, continues these efforts under the aegis of the United Nations, with particular emphasis on combatting communicable diseases and the training of health-care workers.

But despite these accomplishments, much remains to be done in the field of prevention. For too long, we have had a medical care system that is science- and technology-based, focused, essentially, on illness and mortality. It is now patently obvious that both the social and the economic costs of such a system are becoming insupportable.

Implementing prevention—and its corollaries, health education and promotion—is the job of several groups of people:

First, the medical and scientific professions need to continue basic scientific research, and here we are making considerable progress. But increased concern with prevention will also have a decided impact on how primary-care doctors practice medicine. With a shift to health-based rather than morbidity-based medicine, the role of the "new physician" will include a healthy dose of patient education.

Second, practitioners of the social and behavioral sciences—psychologists, economists, city planners—along with lawyers, business leaders, and government officials—must solve the practical and ethical dilemmas confronting us: poverty, crime, civil rights, literacy, education, employment, housing, sanitation, environmental protection, health care delivery systems, and so forth. All of these issues affect public health.

Third is the public at large. We'll consider that very important group in a moment.

Fourth, and the linchpin in this effort, is the public health profession—doctors, epidemiologists, teachers—who must harness the professional expertise of the first two groups and the common sense and cooperation of the third, the public. They must define the problems statistically and qualitatively and then help us set priorities for finding the solutions.

To a very large extent, improving those statistics is the responsibility of every individual. So let's consider more specifically what the role of the individual should be and why health education is so important to that role. First, and most obviously, individuals can protect themselves from illness and injury and thus minimize their need for professional medical care. They can eat a nutritious diet, get adequate exercise, avoid tobacco, alcohol, and drugs, and take prudent steps to avoid accidents. The proverbial "apple a day keeps the doctor away" is not so far from the truth, after all.

Second, individuals should actively participate in their own medical care. They should schedule regular medical and dental checkups. Should they develop an illness or injury, they should know when to treat themselves and when to seek professional help. To gain the maximum benefit from any medical treatment that they do require, individuals must become partners in that treatment. For instance, they should understand the effects and side effects of medications. I counsel young physicians that there is no such thing as too much information when talking with patients. But the corollary is the patient must know enough about the nuts and bolts of the healing process to understand what the doctor is telling him. That is at least partially the patient's responsibility.

Education is equally necessary for us to understand the ethical and public policy issues in health care today. Sometimes individuals will encounter these issues in making decisions about their own treatment or that of family members. Other citizens may encounter them as jurors in medical malpractice cases. But we all become involved, indirectly, when we elect our public officials, from school board members to the president. Should surrogate parenting be legal? To what extent is drug testing desirable, legal, or necessary? Should there be public funding for family planning, hospitals, various types of medical research, and medical care for the indigent? How should we allocate scant technological resources, such as kidney dialysis and organ transplants? What is the proper role of government in protecting the rights of patients?

What are the broad goals of public health in the United States today? In 1980, the Public Health Service issued a report aptly entitled *Promoting Health-Preventing Disease: Objectives for the Nation.* This report expressed its goals in terms of mortality and in terms of intermediate goals in education and health improvement. It identified 15 major concerns: controlling high blood pressure; improving family planning; improving pregnancy care and infant health; increasing the rate of immunization; controlling sexually transmitted diseases; controlling the presence of toxic agents and radiation in the environment; improving occupational safety and health; preventing accidents; promoting water fluoridation and dental health; controlling infectious diseases; decreasing smoking; decreasing alcohol and drug abuse; improving nutrition; promoting physical fitness and exercise; and controlling stress and violent behavior.

For healthy adolescents and young adults (ages 15 to 24), the specific goal was a 20% reduction in deaths, with a special focus on motor vehicle injuries and alcohol and drug abuse. For adults (ages 25 to 64), the aim was 25% fewer deaths, with a concentration on heart attacks, strokes, and cancers.

Smoking is perhaps the best example of how individual behavior can have a direct impact on health. Today cigarette smoking is recognized as the most important single preventable cause of death in our society. It is responsible for more cancers and more cancer deaths than any other known agent; is a prime risk factor for heart and blood vessel disease, chronic bronchitis, and emphysema; and is a frequent cause of complications in pregnancies and of babies born prematurely, underweight, or with potentially fatal respiratory and cardiovascular problems.

Since the release of the Surgeon General's first report on smoking in 1964, the proportion of adult smokers has declined substantially, from 43% in 1965 to 30.5% in 1985. Since 1965, 37 million people have quit smoking. Although there is still much work to be done if we are to become a "smoke-free society," it is heartening to note that public health and public education efforts—such as warnings on cigarette packages and bans on broadcast advertising—have already had significant effects.

In 1835, Alexis de Tocqueville, a French visitor to America, wrote, "In America the passion for physical well-being is general." Today, as then, health and fitness are front-page items. But with the greater scientific and technological resources now available to us, we are in a far stronger position to make good health care available to everyone. And with the greater technological threats to us as we approach the 21st century, the need to do so is more urgent than ever before. Comprehensive information about basic biology, preventive medicine, medical and surgical treatments, and related ethical and public policy issues can help you arm yourself with the knowledge you need to be healthy throughout your life.

FOREWORD

Dale C. Garell, M.D.

Advances in our understanding of health and disease during the 20th century have been truly remarkable. Indeed, it could be argued that modern health care is one of the greatest accomplishments in all of human history. In the early 1900s, improvements in sanitation, water treatment, and sewage disposal reduced death rates and increased longevity. Previously untreatable illnesses can now be managed with antibiotics, immunizations, and modern surgical techniques. Discoveries in the fields of immunology, genetic diagnosis, and organ transplantation are revolutionizing the prevention and treatment of disease. Modern medicine is even making inroads against cancer and heart disease, two of the leading causes of death in the United States.

Although there is much to be proud of, medicine continues to face enormous challenges. Science has vanquished diseases such as smallpox and polio, but new killers, most notably AIDS, confront us. Moreover, we now victimize ourselves with what some have called "diseases of choice," or those brought on by drug and alcohol abuse, bad eating habits, and mismanagement of the stresses and strains of contemporary life. The very technology that is doing so much to prolong life has brought with it previously unimaginable ethical dilemmas related to issues of death and dying. The rising cost of health-care is a matter of central concern to us all. And violence in the form of automobile accidents, homicide, and suicide remain the major killers of young adults.

In the past, most people were content to leave health care and medical treatment in the hands of professionals. But since the 1960s, the consumer of medical care—that is, the patient—has assumed an increasingly central role in the management of his or her own health. There has also been a new emphasis placed on prevention: People are recognizing that their own actions can help prevent many of the conditions that have caused death and disease in the past. This accounts for the growing commitment to good nutrition and regular exercise, for the fact that more and more people are choosing not to smoke, and for a new moderation in people's drinking habits.

People want to know more about themselves and their own health. They are curious about their body: its anatomy, physiology, and biochemistry. They want to keep up with rapidly evolving medical technologies and procedures. They are willing to educate themselves about common disorders and diseases so that they can be full partners in their own health-care.

The ENCYCLOPEDIA OF HEALTH is designed to provide the basic knowledge that readers will need if they are to take significant responsibility for their own health. It is also meant to serve as a frame of reference for further study and exploration. The ENCYCLOPEDIA is divided into five subsections: The Healthy Body; The Life Cycle; Medical Disorders & Their Treatment; Psychological Disorders & Their Treatment; and Medical Issues. For each topic covered by the ENCYCLOPEDIA, we present the essential facts about the relevant biology; the symptoms, diagnosis, and treatment of common diseases and disorders; and ways in which you can prevent or reduce the severity of health problems when that is possible. The ENCYCLOPEDIA also projects what may lie ahead in the way of future treatment or prevention strategies.

The broad range of topics and issues covered in the ENCYCLOPEDIA reflects the fact that human health encompasses physical, psychological, social, environmental, and spiritual well-being. Just as the mind and the body are inextricably linked, so, too, is the individual an integral part of the wider world that comprises his or her family, society, and environment. To discuss health in its broadest aspect it is necessary to explore the many ways in which it is connected to such fields as law, social science, public policy, economics, and even religion. And so, the ENCYCLOPEDIA is meant to be a bridge between science, medical technology, the world at large, and you. I hope that it will inspire you to pursue in greater depth particular areas of interest, and that you will take advantage of the suggestions for further reading and the lists of resources and organizations that can provide additional information.

CHAPTER 1

· · · · · · · · · · · · · · · · · ·

TO A LONG AND HEALTHY LIFE

Clench your fist and imagine it to be a small pump that weighs less than half a pound. Now picture this pump with enough power to push 2,000 gallons of a fairly thick liquid through more than 60,000 miles of tubing every day for 80 or 90 years. The pump you are imagining must have perfect timing and efficiency, never losing pace for more than half a second at any time.

This pump must work 24 hours a day, with twice the power of the arm muscle of a champion heavyweight boxer. It must contract and relax about 70 times a minute, or about 37 million times each year. This pump must be able to start itself with its own built-in electrical impulse and produce enough energy in one hour to raise a medium-sized car three feet off the ground.

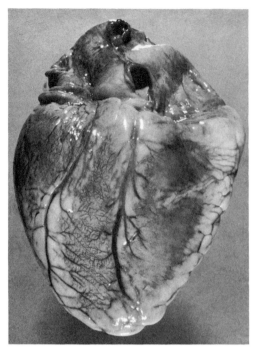

A healthy human heart. The heart must pump 2,000 gallons of blood through 60,000 miles of blood vessels each day.

This extraordinary structure is the human heart. With its chambers, valves, electrical system, tubing, and blood material, the heart is the body's key to survival. Its beat, which begins six months before birth, is the very core of existence, and its efficiency will help determine the quality, as well as the length, of any human life. But despite its strength and consistency, the heart is both fragile and vulnerable. Many things can affect this organ, and many things can go wrong with it. In the United States alone, almost 17 million people—about 7% of the population—have a damaged heart. One out of every 5 men—and 1 out of 17 women—will suffer a heart attack before the age of 60. Moreover, according to an article entitled "Your Heart: A Survival Guide" in the April 1985 issue of *Science Digest* (published by the American Heart Association) a million Americans die each year of cardiovascular disease.

Causes of Cardiovascular Illness

Cardiovascular disease, or illness of the heart and blood vessels, is the number-one killer in the United States. There are several conditions that cause severe damage to the heart and blood vessels. In some cases, babies are born with a heart that already has defects. These *congenital* (existing from birth) conditions usually involve problems with the flow of blood. Sometimes blood flows in a wrong direction within the heart, and sometimes there are malformed areas within the heart that make it hard for blood to flow. Twenty-five thousand babies in this country are born each year with congenital heart defects.

Of all the heart diseases that may be acquired during a person's life, coronary artery disease (CAD) is the most life threatening. Most cases of CAD are caused by a condition in which fat deposits and other materials harden along the inside walls of blood vessels and slow down or even stop the flow of blood to the heart. When the vessels that lead to the heart become blocked, the heart does not get enough blood to do its job and often cannot keep the body alive. In another form of heart disease, the heart muscle itself becomes weak and cannot continue to pump blood properly.

A very common and very serious circulatory disorder is high blood pressure, one of the major causes of fatal cardiovascular disease. Blood in the body presses against the vessels through which it flows much like water in a garden hose. When the pressure of the blood is too high, the heart must work harder to pump it through the body. This often leads to a very dangerous condition called *hypertension*.

In addition, there are a number of infections that can damage the heart. These conditions can cause inflammation of the muscles that make up the heart or of the layer of tissue that holds the heart steady in the chest. Infection can also damage the valves that control blood flow between parts of the heart.

The blood, with its millions of circulating cells, is also susceptible to a number of serious health problems. The heart pumps three major groups of blood cells to the rest of the body: red blood cells, which are oxygen carriers; white cells, which are disease fighters; and platelets, which are blood clotters. If any of these groups of cells fail to function properly, the body may be seriously affected. Such diseases as leukemia, anemia, and hemophilia are among the most serious blood disorders.

Over the years, medical science has learned a great deal about the heart and circulation. Today, many problems related to the heart and the circulatory system can be detected at an early stage and controlled by new drugs and therapies. The marvels of modern operating technology have made heart surgery a common procedure and heart transplants a familiar reality. And yet, heart disease continues to increase. The number of cases of coronary artery disease rises every year. The harsh fact remains that heart disease is one of the 20th century's major health problems.

Part of the reason for the increase of heart disease lies in the greater longevity of people today. As time passes, the heart is less able to do the work it did in a younger body, and after years of steady beating, the heart is more likely to break down. The encouraging news is that fewer young heart patients now die of cardiovascular diseases. Better hospital care, surgical breakthrough, and more advanced life-support equipment account for some of the lives that are being saved.

Experts believe, however, that the key to leading a longer, healthier life lies in understanding how to reduce the risk of heart disease in the first place. More and more studies are showing a direct relationship between heart disease and smoking, cholesterol, and high blood pressure. Other important risk factors that put an added strain on the heart and that can be reduced through the development of healthy habits include lack of exercise, being overweight, and stress.

An increasing number of cardiovascular diseases are being treated, controlled, and even cured. Many coronary diseases can be prevented, and many lives can be saved, through an understanding of the conditions that place the heart and the blood vessels in danger.

The more you know about the heart, the blood vessels, and the blood itself, the more you will understand about the things that can go wrong with this complicated system. Learning about the problems that affect the circulatory system, and learning about the advances that are being made to keep it in good working order, may help you or someone you care about avoid becoming a candidate for heart disease. Keeping up to date with the latest facts about your heart and blood vessels can be an important step in keeping fit, staying healthy, and living longer.

•　　　•　　　•　　　•

CHAPTER 2

· · · · · · · · · · · · · · · ·

THE HISTORY OF HEART STUDY

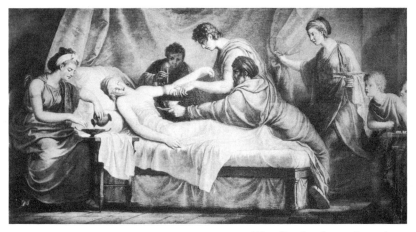

Bloodletting in ancient times

People in almost every culture throughout recorded history have looked upon the heart and the blood as sustainers of life. Many early civilizations believed that blood carried the soul. In many early religions, blood was believed to have the power to hold good and evil spirits within the body. Some farmers sprinkled blood on their seeds to nourish the crops. It was common for early doctors to drain, or "let," blood from patients in order to release the "evil" within them. And ancient Romans, believing that blood would bring good health, drank the blood of dying gladiators in the hope of preserving youth and vigor. And yet, amid so much folklore and superstition, the ancient civilizations had a remarkable—if limited—understanding of circulation.

More than 3,000 years ago the ancient Chinese, who knew that blood was essential to life, wrote about the connection between the heart and the blood. They understood that the flow of blood was continuous and that the heart regulated the flow of the body's blood through blood vessels, but they mistakenly thought that these vessels also carried air, urine, and waste. The writings of Erasistratus, a Greek physician and anatomist who lived more than 2,300 years ago, also show great insight into circulation by clearly describing veins and arteries and tracing them to the heart. But like the Chinese, Erasistratus thought that arteries (which means air ducts) carried air, not blood, through the body.

The most influential and important of these early scientific writers was Galen, a Greek physician from Asia Minor who wrote more than 125 treatises on the body. He was physician to the Roman emperor Marcus Aurelius during the 2nd century A.D. and also ministered to the gladiators at Pergamum, an ancient Greek city in western Asia Minor. From his dissection of apes, Galen learned that the heart is composed of muscle. He also demonstrated that the arteries carry blood, not air. However, Galen's understanding of the circulatory system was imperfect. For example, he believed that blood moved back and forth much like the tides. He also thought that the heart acted as a low-

The Greek physician Galen treating a gladiator. Galen was the first to show that the arteries carry blood, not air, through the body.

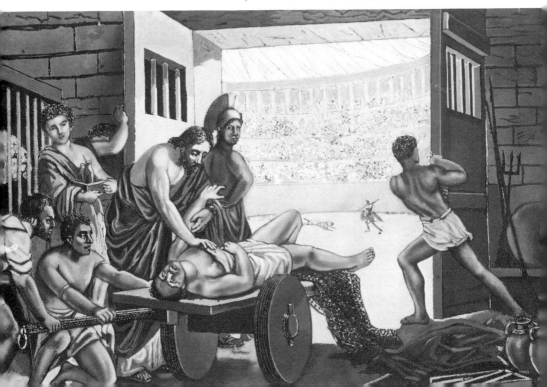

A portrait of Fabricius, who discovered that valves existed in the veins, although he did not understand their function.

temperature oven to keep the blood warm, and that "spirits" existed in the bloodstream. And he held that blood trickled from one side of the heart to the other through tiny pores in the heart.

The Age of the Scientific Revolution

Despite his errors, Galen's theories on the heart and blood were regarded as medical truths until the 17th century, an era that marked a turning point in the entire history of science. During this time, the English doctor and anatomist William Harvey (1578–1657) startled the world with his revolutionary and scientifically demonstrable discoveries about circulation, which were the 17th century's most significant breakthroughs in the fields of physiology and medicine.

Harvey began his circulation studies in 1597 at Italy's great medical learning center the University of Padua. Fifty years earlier at the same institute, Andreas Vesalius (1514–64), a Belgian medical student who was to become known as the Father of Anatomy, performed his dissections. By viewing the thick wall in the heart, Vesalius corrected Galen's theory that pores exist between the two sides of the heart.

Realdo Colombo (1516–59) was Vesalius's successor at Padua. In his experiments with animals, Colombo found that blood flows from the left side of the heart to the arteries, then on to the veins, and returns to the right side of the heart and, finally, the lungs. Fabricius ab Aquapendente, a student of Gabriello Fallopio, who was in turn a student of Vesalius, was William Harvey's professor at Padua. He had found that valves (which he called little doors) existed in the veins, but he did not understand their function. It was with this background of research and inquiry that Harvey began his studies.

In 1602, William Harvey joined the Royal College of Physicians and began to practice medicine in England. As part of his continuing research, Harvey wanted to find out about the route the blood took through the body. He performed experiments on 15 species of animals. These detailed tests supplied some important information.

Etching of William Harvey demonstrating the circulation of a deer's blood to King Charles I of England. Harvey's experiments proved for the first time that blood circulates through the body in a closed system.

When Harvey placed a tight knot around a live animal's artery, he saw that blood accumulated above the knot, on the side nearest the heart. When the artery was cut open on both sides of the knot, blood spurted out of the upper cut. This showed that blood in an artery flows away from the heart. When Harvey tied a knot around a vein in the animal's body, blood swelled below the knot. When he cut open the vein on both sides of the knot, blood trickled out from the cut that was away from the heart. This showed that blood in veins flows toward the heart.

Harvey was fascinated by the tiny vein valves that Fabricius had discovered. Press hard on the inside of your forearm a few inches above the wrist. You will be able to see tiny bumps appear along the bluish vein that runs up the center of your arm. These are the valves that interested William Harvey so many years ago. Pressing on the vein makes the valves in the vein bulge out. When the pressure is released, the bulges remain. They will disappear if the arm is stroked in an upward direction, toward the heart. These one-way valves, which are situated all along the veins, prevent blood that is returning to the heart from flowing backward.

Harvey continued to experiment. He examined the heart of a dead person and measured the amount of water it could hold. Then, he multiplied that amount by the number of heartbeats produced per minute, then estimated how much liquid would be pumped in a day. By simple mathematics, Harvey concluded that the heart must pump the same blood over and over again, in a circle. The body could not possibly contain enough blood unless it was recycling the same blood continuously.

Harvey announced his conclusions in a treatise called *On the Movement of the Heart and Blood in Animals.* His book showed that the heart beats by muscular contraction, squeezing blood into arteries through one-way valves. It also held that blood returned to the heart through veins, and continued its cyclical journey again and again. It took Harvey 20 years to find a printer who would publish his theories, for few people were impressed by—or even believed—his findings. Finally, in 1628, Harvey printed his findings, in Latin, in Frankfurt, Germany, where he thought they would be better received than in his own country. Eventually Harvey's ideas were accepted; indeed, his work came to be recognized as among the most important in the history of medicine.

Progress Continues

During Harvey's lifetime the development of the microscope was in its infancy, and so he never saw the miniature blood vessels, or capillaries, that connect the arteries and the veins. He thought that there were small spaces in the body's tissue through which blood passed on its way from artery to vein. It was not until 1661, four years after Harvey's death, that Marcello Malpighi (1628–94) became the first person to see capillaries. Malpighi, who had studied at the University of Bologna, in Italy, was then a professor and experimenter. He used a simple microscope to discover the connecting blood vessels that had escaped William Harvey.

The tool Malpighi used—a microscope—was constructed by Antoni van Leeuwenhoek (1632–1723), a Dutch cloth merchant who used his spare time to make magnifying lenses. He developed lenses that were powerful enough to see the shape of blood cells. These lenses were so strong that Leeuwenhoek was able to observe blood circulating in the web of a frog's foot and blood cells inside the capillaries of a tadpole's tail. The lenses showed a whole world of microscopic animals, which Leeuwenhoek called "little beasties."

In this same decade, the 1660s, Jean-Baptiste Denis (1643–1704), a French philosopher, mathematician, and court physician to King Louis XIV, began some historic experiments. He used a short tube and a warm environment to transfuse blood successfully from the leg artery of one dog to the body of another.

In 1667, Denis came upon a 16-year-old boy who was very weak with a high fever. The boy had been bled several times in attempts to cure him, was lethargic, and had no appetite. Denis transfused some lamb's blood into the youngster, which temporarily brought him into a cheerful, restored state. The youngster survived. Unfortunately, when Denis tried this same procedure on another patient, the patient died shortly thereafter.

Despite the fatality rate, some people thought that transfusions of animal blood could cure madness and other severe conditions, as well as aging. In 1678, the French government passed laws prohibiting blood transfusions—legislation that would remain in effect for nearly 150 years.

During the late 1600s, the fascinating universe of circulation was arousing the interest of many physicians. In Dublin, Ireland, Dr. Allen Moulin experimented with sheep, dogs, rabbits, and

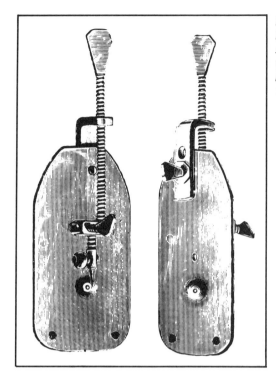

Drawings of Antoni van Leeuwenhoek's microscope, the lenses of which were unsurpassed in efficiency until the 19th century.

ducks. He proved that blood makes up about $^1/_{20}$ of the weight of the body. By the middle of the next century, Stephen Hales (1677–1761), the English clergyman and physiologist, had discovered the existence of blood pressure and its importance to good health. Hales was able to put a glass tube into the artery of a horse to measure the pressure of a column of blood.

In 1785 William Withering (1741–99), an English doctor, published his findings on the foxglove plant, which botanists know as *Digitalis purpurea*. Foxglove tea had been used by an old English woman to relieve dropsy, a condition in which fluids collect in body tissue. Withering showed how the leaves of this plant could be used to make a medication that slowed the pulse rate of the heart. It was known that dropsy was caused in part by heart disease. Clots and damaged valves can cause fluid to collect in body tissue. Increasing heart contractions can relieve this condition. *Digitalis* slows the heart rate and increases the force of contraction. If heart muscles move more powerfully, it decreases both the pressure in the bloodstream and the volume of blood in the heart chambers and increases the flow of blood to the kidneys; this last action leads to better urine output and reduced dropsy. This medicine, digitalis, was the first and is still the most important medicine used in treating the heart. In fact, other heart medications were developed from this same plant during the 20th century.

As the 19th century began, more heart study continued. In 1816, Dr. René T. H. Laënnec (1781–1826), a French physician, had trouble hearing the heartbeats of an overweight woman he was examining. In order to block out other sounds, he rolled up paper into a tube and held it to her chest. Later, Laënnec fashioned a hollow wooden stick to help him listen to his patients' heart. This instrument was flared at one end and had an earpiece at the other. Laënnec had made the first *stethoscope,* a term that means "to view the chest."

Around this time, another Englishman, Dr. James Blundell, began to transfuse human blood to mothers after childbirth. He used a pump, a syringe, and a funnel to push blood into his

German bacteriologist Paul Ehrlich, who settled a dispute over which agent fights diseases in the body when he discovered that antitoxins and white blood cells work together to do so.

patients and was able to save 11 out of 15 women from *hemor-rhaging* (bleeding profusely). What is remarkable about Blundell's success is that in his time there was no knowledge of blood-typing. The discovery of blood groups was still almost 100 years away. Blundell was lucky that the 11 women did not die of cross-typing. (The transfused blood may have been type O—see Chapter 4.) Had typing been known, Blundell might have transfused more women in complete safety.

As the 19th century drew to a close, Élie Metchnikoff (1845–1916), a Russian scientist, discovered the existence of white blood cells and their ability to devour germs. At the same time, a German researcher, Emil von Behring (1854–1917), discovered antitoxins, which are chemical compounds in the blood that also help to protect the body against disease. A dispute arose between these two men, each arguing that he had discovered the agent that fights disease in the body.

In 1903, Paul Ehrlich (1854–1915), a German bacteriologist, settled the dispute. Ehrlich found that the antitoxins in the blood prepare bacteria for attack by white cells. They break down the protective armor that bacteria possess. He concluded that both men were right: Antitoxins and white blood cells worked together.

The Twentieth Century

As heart study entered the 20th century, no one could have predicted the great advances that were to come. Most physicians at this time still believed that the heart was out of bounds. It was the common belief that the heart could not be surgically treated. Doctors felt that any cut to the heart would result in death. But a small number of cases indicated that the heart could be punctured without death resulting. In 1896, Dr. Ludwig Rehn, a German surgeon, stitched up a wound in the heart of a 22-year-old woman. A year later, a Dr. Tuffier successfully treated a case of cardiac arrest with a hand massage.

The new century was a promising one for heart research. The first blood-pressure cuff, which wrapped around the arm to measure pressure, had been invented a few years before the century began. In 1901, Karl Landsteiner (1868–1943), the naturalized American immunologist and pathologist, announced the discovery of the four blood groups. It would take another 10 years for donors and patients to have their blood typed for transfusion and another 29 years for Dr. Landsteiner to receive a Nobel Prize for his work, but the century was off to a good start.

In 1909 a new transfusion tube had been developed, and by 1914, blood could be transfused from a bottle. This came about because of the work of an Argentinian doctor named Luis Agote, who discovered that sodium citrate would stop blood from clotting when it left the body. In the mid-1920s, Russian researchers had discovered that citrated blood could be stored in refrigerators at 40 degrees Fahrenheit. This meant that a donor could leave his blood for later use.

The 1920s heralded a series of tremendous breakthroughs. In a landmark case, American surgeons E. Cutler and S. A. Levine successfully operated on the defective heart valve of an 11-year-old girl. Two years later, Henry Houttar, a British surgeon, performed the first successful operation to remove blockage from a heart valve.

In 1923 Dr. Willem Einthoven (1860–1927), a Dutch doctor, received the Nobel Prize for his work in the development of the electrocardiograph (EKG), which makes tracings of the heart's electrical activity. These tracings show patterns of waves and peaks as the heart contracts and relaxes. Abnormal heart conditions change these patterns. The EKG tells whether the heartbeat is even or irregular, how long the heart rests between beats, and can show the doctor any overworked, injured, or dead cardiac muscle. To this day it remains one of the most important tools that doctors use for diagnosing heart problems.

In 1929, a German surgeon, Werner Forssmann (1904–79), performed a daring and heroic experiment. He examined the inside of his own heart by threading a small hollow tube, called a *catheter*, directly into his arm vein, then extending it 20 inches to his heart. Forssmann believed that this technique, now called *cardiac catheterization*, would be an important tool for diagnosing circulation problems. With no other doctor willing to assist him, Forssmann, watched by his nurse, inserted the catheter by using a mirror and a fluoroscope, a machine that enabled him to see the shadows of his heart and blood vessels. Because he felt that others would not believe what he had done, Forssmann walked down the hall and up two flights of stairs in order to be photographed in an X-ray lab with the tube still inside his body.

Dr. Willem Einthoven, who was awarded the Nobel Prize in 1923 for his work in the development of the electro-cardiograph.

Today, this procedure is widely used to inject dyes for X rays, to take blood samples, to measure pressure, and to examine the structure of the heart.

Open Heart Surgery

Several important developments occurred during the late 1930s and early 1940s. In 1939, Dr. Robert Gross of Harvard Medical School performed the first successful surgery to correct a congenital heart defect. Dr. Gross was able to close a duct in a seven-year-old girl's heart and allow blood to leak from the body's largest artery to another artery leading to the lungs, when it was needed.

In 1944, Dr. John Blalock of Johns Hopkins University used the first bypass procedure. The patient was a blue baby, a newborn infant born with bluish tint because of oxygen-poor blood.

Dr. Blalock saved the baby's life by providing an alternate route for blood that could not get through a blocked blood vessel.

By 1950, the stage was being set for open-heart surgery, where the heart itself would be under repair. Until this time, major surgical procedures had not been performed on the heart. Surgeons could work around the heart, or near it. They could operate on exposed regions of the heart, or on arteries and veins leading to and from the heart. But they could not do more than that surgery on an organ that was beating approximately 72 times each minute and keeping the patient alive.

In order to repair the heart itself, the organ would have to be slowed down or temporarily replaced. Wilfred Bigelow, in Canada, used a cooling method to slow the heart rate of experimental animals from 180 beats per minute to 25. This process can be accomplished through the use of drugs, by passing the blood through a cooling tube, or by placing the patient in an ice-filled

Dr. Christiaan Barnard in 1967, the year he and his surgical team performed the first successful heart transplant.

tub, which was the method that Bigelow used. The procedure is a dangerous one because slowing the heart rate can cause brain damage as well as irregular twitching of the heart muscle.

Still, major advances continued. But the real breakthrough in open-heart surgery came in the form of the heart-lung machine. John Gibbon, an American professor of surgery, his wife, and others built an experimental machine to do the work of the patient's heart and lungs. It would pump blood and supply oxygen to the body during an operation, giving the doctor valuable time needed for delicate heart surgery. In 1954, Dr. Gibbon used his heart-lung machine during an operation on an 18-year-old girl. Today, this machine is a standard fixture in heart surgery.

Microsurgery and Spare Parts

The 1960s brought more milestones in heart research. In New York, Dr. Adrian Kantorowicz perfected a battery-powered pacemaker, a light electrical device that could regulate the heart rate. Heart surgeons perfected the carotid bypass, a surgical procedure to divert more blood to the brain and ward off the danger of fatal strokes. And *microsurgery* became a familiar word.

In 1957, Dr. Julius Jacobson, a vascular surgeon at the University of Vermont Medical School, began using jeweler's tools to stitch tiny blood vessels that measured only a millimeter in diameter. By the late 1960s, precision instruments were in common use in extremely minute and delicate heart and blood-vessel surgery. Such microsurgery is now easily done on the walls of arteries that are in danger of leaking or bursting. The survival rate of this type of surgery is now up to 90%.

The closing years of the 1960s will be recorded in the history of heart study as the most dramatic and momentous since the discoveries of William Harvey. On December 3, 1967, Dr. Christiaan Barnard of South Africa transplanted a human heart into the body of Louis Washansky. Although the recipient of the world's first "successful" human-heart transplant lived for only 18 days, a milestone had been reached. On January 1, 1968, Dr. Barnard performed a similar operation on a 58-year-old dentist, Dr. Philip Blaiberg. Dr. Blaiberg survived for 593 days with a heart that at one time had beat in the chest of another human being. Today, 4,000 people in the United States are living with another person's heart in their chest, and 85% of them live for more than a year:

The longest-surviving recipient of a heart transplant is still doing well almost 19 years after receiving his new heart.

On December 2, 1982, the next, inevitable step was taken. Dr. Barney Clark was given the first permanent artificial heart by Dr. William De Vries at the University of Utah's College of Medicine. The Jarvik-7 heart was designed by Dr. Robert Jarvik at the Division of Artificial Organs in Salt Lake City. It kept Dr. Clark alive for 112 days.

Admittedly, many of those 112 days were difficult. The patient with an artificial heart must remain wired to a compressor that operates the heart. Dr. Clark developed seizures, bubbles in his lung, and kidney failure. And yet, survival with an artificial heart, although limited and problematic, bodes well for many patients. The Jarvik-7 heart is the only hope to many people for whom a transplant donor has not yet been found.

As with any science, today's knowledge of the heart and blood vessels is tomorrow's history. It is less than a century since physicians regarded the heart as an untouchable organ. There is little doubt that further study and research will bring even greater knowledge. The history of heart study has shown that such knowledge and its application will serve to prolong the efficiency of this intricate and life-supporting system of circulation.

•   •   •   •

CHAPTER 3

. . . .

UNDERSTANDING THE HEART AND BLOOD VESSELS

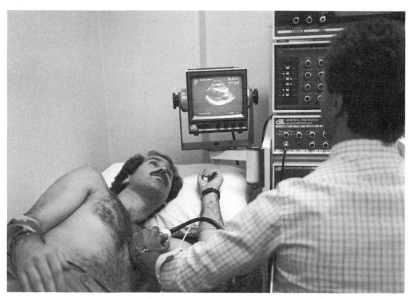

Heart sonogram

In order for the body to stay alive, each of its cells must receive a continuous supply of food and oxygen. At the same time, carbon dioxide and other materials produced by the cells must be picked up for removal from the body. The heart and its network of blood vessels are able to circulate the raw materials for the energy that powers every thought and action of the body. At the same time, this transport system efficiently relieves each cell of its unwanted wastes. By doing this job over and over, every minute of every hour of every day, the heart and blood vessels serve to keep the cells, and in this way the body, alive and well for a lifetime.

The circulatory system, with its several circuits and 60,000 miles of intricate passageways, is not very different from a major highway system in any busy metropolis. The life of a city may depend upon its system of roadways, along which the supplies and services needed by its people are transported. Similarly, the human body depends a great deal upon a properly functioning circulatory system. Like the traffic on a busy highway, the blood in the body's vessels must keep moving to its destination, then return to its starting point and move out again. Any discussion of the intricacy of the human circulatory system must begin with its master organ: the heart.

A LOOK AT THE HEART

The human heart is approximately the size of a grown person's fist. In an average adult, this pear-shaped organ is about five and a half inches long and about three and a half inches across, and it weighs less than a pound.

The heart is attached to the breastbone by special connective tissues called ligaments. It seems to hang fairly high in the middle of the chest cavity, between the lungs, with its lower end, or *apex*, pointing left. The apex pulses with every beat of the heart. This is what you feel if you hold your hand to your chest. The pulsing of the apex sometimes can be seen if the heart is pounding, or beating, very rapidly. The location of this pulsing part of the heart has led some people to believe incorrectly that the heart is on the left side of the body.

The heart is made of a special kind of muscle tissue that is not found anywhere else in the body. At first glance this *cardiac* (heart) muscle looks like another, more common muscle tissue— the striped, or striated, tissue found in voluntary muscles. Voluntary muscles, such as those that move the arms and legs, respond to a person's will. A closer look shows that unlike the separated fibers of voluntary muscles, each fiber in cardiac muscle is connected to other fibers on either side. As a result, any signal sent to these muscles is received by the whole heart at the same time. Cardiac muscle also is unusual because it needs less rest between work periods than other muscle tissue, and because wastes do not build up the same way as they do in other muscles.

The mass of cardiac muscles that is the heart is enclosed in a double bag, or sac. The inner sac fits tightly around the heart

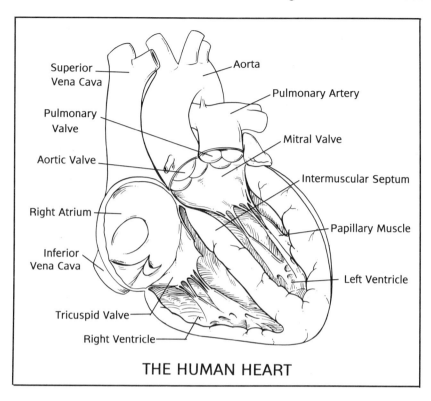

Superior Vena Cava

Aorta

Pulmonary Artery

Pulmonary Valve

Mitral Valve

Aortic Valve

Intermuscular Septum

Right Atrium

Papillary Muscle

Inferior Vena Cava

Left Ventricle

Tricuspid Valve

Right Ventricle

THE HUMAN HEART

and is attached to it. At the apex, it folds over on itself and forms an outer sac. This sac fits loosely over the heart, except at the top, or *base*. Here it is attached to the large blood vessels that stem from the heart. Both the inner and the outer sacs form the *pericardium*, a Latin term for "around the heart." In between the two sacs of the pericardium is a thin fluid that keeps the heart's muscle surfaces smooth and lubricated. This liquid also supports the heart and cushions it as it beats.

The walls of the heart are made of thick muscle that is twisted into rings and loops. Lining the walls is a smooth thin layer of cells called the *endocardium*. This lining helps to reduce any friction that may be caused by blood that is constantly moving through the four hollow chambers of the heart.

Each chamber of the heart has its own special job. The left atrium and the right atrium are the heart's upper, or receiving, chambers. The word *atrium* means "entrance hall" in Latin. The left and right ventricles are the lower, or pumping, chambers. *Ventricle* is the Latin word for "little belly." Blood can enter the heart only through the upper atria and can leave the heart only through the lower ventricles.

A solid wall of thick muscle called the *septum* separates the left and right sides of the heart. These two sides do not interact with each other; rather, each pumps blood separately, and they can even be considered two separate hearts. The "left heart," which pumps oxygen-rich blood to the entire body, is the larger and stronger one. The wall of the left ventricle is three or four times thicker than that of the right ventricle, because it must do five times as much work.

The flow of blood from the upper chambers to the lower chambers of the heart is controlled by valves. The *tricuspid valve*, named for its three flaps, or cusps, lies between the right atrium and the right ventricle. The *mitral valve*, which resembles a bishop's miter, or cap, lies between the left atrium and the left ventricle. These valves are able to prevent blood from flowing backward. They shut tightly to keep blood from flowing from a lower chamber to an upper chamber. Each ventricle has an additional valve at the point where blood leaves to enter a major blood vessel. These larger valves prevent blood that is leaving the heart from flowing back into the lower chambers.

THE HEART AT WORK

The heart must pump about 2,000 gallons of blood each day through 2 major (and several minor) circulation routes in the body. To do this, the heart beats, or contracts and relaxes, an average of about 70 times per minute. No one really knows how the heart beats. All other muscles in the body have some nerve connection to the brain. In this way the brain is able to send directions for movement to the muscle. Surprisingly, the heart, the master muscle of the body, has no such link to the central nervous system.

In the upper part of the right atrium there is a small patch of special heart tissue unlike any other in the body. This minute matter, known as the *sinus node* or the *sinoatrial node*, is the heart's pacemaker. Somehow, it is able to start a heartbeat every $8/_{10}$ of a second throughout a person's life. The brain is able to change the rate of the heart, but it is the mysterious node that triggers the beat and establishes its pace. This group of cells works independently from the rest of the body; even when the heart is removed from the body altogether, it signals the heart to go on beating as long as it has blood to pump.

The group of cells in the sinus node sends out a tiny electrical current 60 or 70 times a minute. This current spreads along the walls of both atria to another node in the bottom left-hand corner of the right atrium, close to the septum. From these the electrical signal travels to a cluster of nerve fibers, called the *Bundle of His* (after the Swiss physiologist Wilhelm His [1863–1934], who first described them), then down the inside of the ventricles, and finally back up the outer ventricle walls. This electric current, which spreads from the inside of the heart wall to the outside, causes a contraction, or shortening, of the heart muscle, which we know as the heartbeat.

When the heart beats, the muscles at the top of the heart contract first. The squeeze that occurs in the atria ripples downward to the lower chambers. However, the wave motion of the heart's contraction travels so rapidly that the millions of thin strands of heart muscle seem to contract all at once. After each contraction, both chambers rest for $4/_{10}$ of a second. Because the cardiac cycle takes place roughly every $8/_{10}$ of a second, the heart actually rests for half its working time.

During contractions, the chambers of the heart shorten and harden, just as they lengthen and enlarge during the times of relaxation. With each contraction, blood is pumped in squirts from the heart's upper chambers to its lower chambers and from the lower chambers into large blood vessels. In between beats, when the heart is at rest, the atria fill up with the fresh blood that will be pumped out with the next heartbeat.

The heart of the average man beats 70 times a minute. The average woman has a heart rate of 78 per minute. However, heart rates vary from person to person. Many conditions can affect the rate of the heart: the climate, the position of the body, the activity of the person, the food being eaten, and even a person's mood. Groups of nerves in the brain control the speed of the heart rate. They slow down the heart when less blood is needed and speed it up when the cells need extra oxygen.

The heart can adjust the amount of blood it pumps at any given time. During heavy exercise, the heart may pump eight times as much blood as when it is relaxed. If there are great short-term demands by the body for more blood, the muscles of the heart can thicken. The chambers can enlarge to as much as double their original size.

A heartbeat can be felt, but it cannot be heard. The sounds that are heard when the ear or a stethoscope is placed to the chest are caused by the heart's valves. The normal, rhythmic contraction of the heart, or *systole,* is followed by the closing of the valves between the upper and lower chambers of the heart. The heart's relaxation, or *diastole,* is followed by the shutting of the valves that lead to blood vessels. Both sets of valves produce a distinct sound as they ward off a return flow of blood. If we think of the heart as producing a repeating "flub/dub, flub/dub" sound, the "flub" is made by the valves that close between the atria and the ventricles. The "dub" is the closing of the valves between the ventricles and the blood vessels.

The uninterrupted beating of the heart is a constant reassurance that blood is being propelled to the body's waiting cells. The contracting and relaxing of the heart mark the beginning of a journey through thousands of miles of blood vessels that help to push the blood toward its destination and return it efficiently to its starting point.

A LOOK AT BLOOD VESSELS

Blood vessels are tubes that carry blood to and from all parts of the body. They are somewhat like a water supply system that begins with a large central main and branches into smaller and smaller pipes as it delivers water to individual homes. Unlike the metal pipes that make up a water-delivery system, blood vessels are soft and elastic. They are able to change their shape and are made up of living tissue.

The human circulatory system is made up of three types of blood vessel. *Arteries* and smaller *arterioles* are vessels that carry blood away from the heart; *veins* and smaller *venules* transport blood back to the heart; and finally, microscopic *capillaries* link the tiniest veins and arteries.

Arteries are composed of three coats. The inside layer is called the *intima* and is made of flat, smooth cells that face inward. The intima has another thin layer of loose fibers that is continuous with the endocardium, the heart's own inner lining.

The middle layer of the artery, or the *media,* is the thickest one. It is made of elastic tissue and muscle fibers arranged so that they run around the tube. Large arteries must have lots of

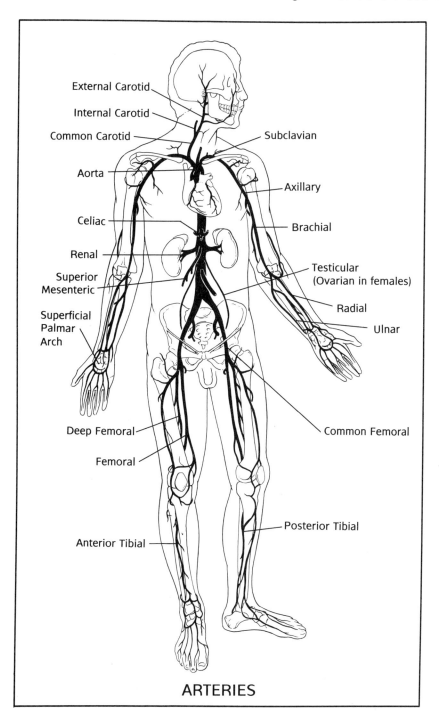

External Carotid

Internal Carotid

Common Carotid

Subclavian

Aorta

Axillary

Celiac

Brachial

Renal

Superior
Mesenteric

Testicular
(Ovarian in females)

Radial

Superficial
Palmar
Arch

Ulnar

Deep Femoral

Common Femoral

Femoral

Posterior Tibial

Anterior Tibial

ARTERIES

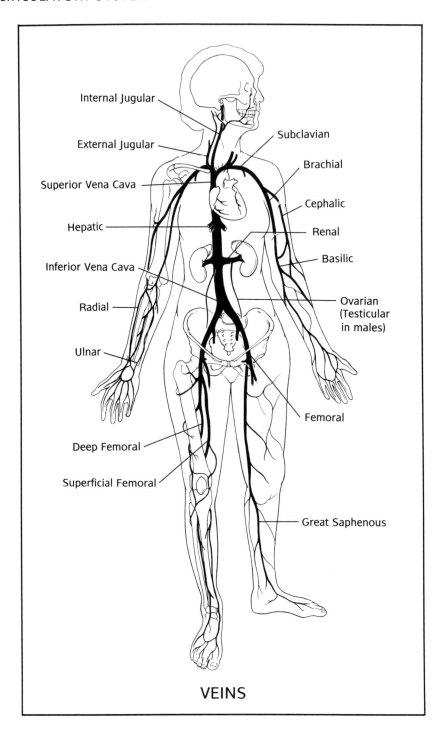

Internal Jugular

External Jugular

Superior Vena Cava

Hepatic

Inferior Vena Cava

Radial

Ulnar

Deep Femoral

Superficial Femoral

Subclavian

Brachial

Cephalic

Renal

Basilic

Ovarian
(Testicular
in males)

Femoral

Great Saphenous

VEINS

give. They stretch like rubber bands, stay stretched for an instant, and then relax between heartbeats. This movement is called a *pulse* and can be felt easily in the wrist, at the side of the neck and the forehead, and behind the knee. It is really a ripple over the surface of the arteries, which travels very quickly and is felt a split second after the heartbeat.

The outside layer, or *adventitia,* is a mesh of strong fibers and connective tissue. The two surrounding layers support the important muscle tissue of the inner media. The walls of arterioles must be able to open and close in order to divert blood to where it is most needed. The skin of a person who is doing something active such as exercise or sport is often pink, or ruddy, as the walls of the small arteries open wide to supply more blood to arm and leg muscles. The skin of that same person may become pale and cool while he or she is studying. This happens when arterioles carrying blood to the skin begin to narrow, so that a greater amount of blood can be rerouted to the brain.

The largest artery in the body stems directly from the left ventricle of the heart. This is the *aorta,* which is about one inch in diameter and curves in a great arch up from the heart, down along the spine, and into the abdomen. Arteries that branch from the aorta deliver blood to the head, the digestive organs, and to the arms and legs.

The *pulmonary,* or lung artery, is the circulatory system's other main artery, and it stems from the heart's right ventricle. It carries blood away from the heart and delivers it to the lungs. Both the aorta and the pulmonary artery work with the help of the valves that are between them and the ventricles from which they stem. As blood is pumped into these large arteries, the valves shut tight like a pair of swinging doors that open only one way. In this way, the blood cannot flow back into the heart's lower chambers.

Veins, which transport blood back to the heart, have walls that are thinner than those of the arteries. Although the veins also have three coats, or layers, they are made of less muscle and more strands of white fiber. The walls of the veins are also more rigid than those of arteries. When we describe arteries, we usually begin with the largest arteries and observe how they branch into smaller vessels. Veins, on the other hand, begin at the capillaries and branch out into larger and larger veins as they approach the heart. The two largest branches of veins are the superior and inferior *venae cavae*, which lie, respectively, just above and below the heart.

Blood in the arteries has been pumped by the heart and is therefore pushed directly as it moves along its route. Fluid in the veins, on the other hand, is on a return trip. To give this blood an extra push forward, veins are equipped with small valves, or little pockets, with open ends that face the heart. These valves are so important that they can be found every half inch along the veins of the legs. As the pockets of the valves fill with returning blood, the valves close and shut off part of the vein. Then, muscles in the veins contract and help push the blood on its way. The valves also make certain that the blood in the veins will never flow backward.

Together with the arteries and the veins, the capillaries make up the 60,000-mile network of the body's blood vessels. The capillaries are the body's tiniest and most abundant blood vessels. One hundred twenty short capillaries would measure just three inches in length, and all the body's capillaries laid end to end would circle the equator twice. Capillaries link arterioles and venules and serve as points of interchange for oxygen, food, and wastes. The walls of these vessels must therefore be thin enough for some materials from the blood and the cells to pass through.

A magnified view of red blood cells in a capillary of the spinal cord. Capillaries are points of interchange for oxygen, food, and waste.

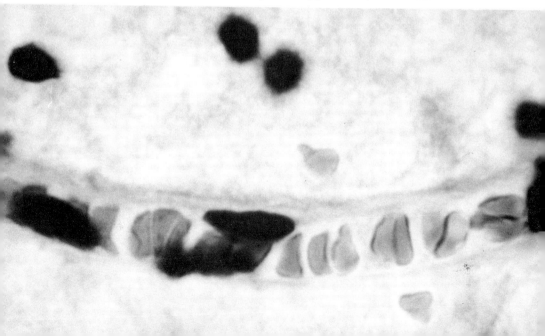

THE PATHS OF CIRCULATION

As mentioned earlier, the human heart, with its four chambers, is really two hearts. Each heart is in charge of a major route of circulation. The left heart controls the general, or *systemic*, route of circulation. Systemic circulation, which delivers blood to and from the body parts, has several local routes. In this local system, special circuits deliver blood to the kidney, to the liver, to the brain, and to the heart itself. The right heart is in charge of *pulmonary* circulation, which delivers blood to and from the lungs. In total, five quarts of blood are pumped through the intricate circulatory paths every minute. These paths are elaborate, but so efficient that the entire process of circulation in both systems, during which every cell in the body is serviced, takes only a total of 20 seconds.

A system that is routed in a circuit has no particular beginning. Because any point in the path of circulation can serve as a place in which to begin the journey of blood through the body, we have chosen an arbitrary starting point: the right atrium, which has filled with oxygen-poor blood during the heart's split-second relaxation.

The journey begins as the right atrium, filled with newly entered blood, contracts. This movement forces the blood from this upper chamber into the right ventricle, which now contracts and forces the flaps of the tricuspid valve into a horizontal position. As the ends of the flaps meet, they shut off the opening into the right atrium, preventing any backward flow of blood. The contraction of the right ventricle also swings open the valves that lead to the pulmonary artery, and the blood is now pumped out of the heart.

The pulmonary artery branches toward the left and right lungs, and the blood is moved into smaller and smaller arterioles until it branches into the capillaries that meet the air sacs of the lungs. At the capillaries, blood cells pick up oxygen and deposit excess carbon dioxide and water vapor. The newly oxygenated red blood now moves into tiny venules that will lead it back to the heart. The venules branch into larger and larger veins. Finally, the blood is directed into pulmonary veins that fill the left atrium of the heart. Now the aerated blood is ready for distribution into the rest of the body.

Once again, the blood is squeezed from an upper chamber, this time in the left heart, to the left ventricle. A contraction of the left ventricle, the largest and strongest chamber, pumps the blood into the aorta. This contraction activates the mitral valve between the two chambers and swings open the valve in the aorta. Blood enters the aorta under great pressure. As in any pump-driven system, the pressure is greatest nearest the pump. If the aorta were opened, blood would spurt out in a column five to six feet high. Even though the blood is pumped in squirts, it flows smoothly in the arteries. The elastic walls of the aorta balloon out as blood enters, and some blood is delayed in the stretched vessel. When the aorta walls spring back, the blood is propelled forward more smoothly and continues to flow in a stream.

Once it is in the arteries, the blood is on its way through smaller arteries and arterioles to the capillaries that border on every cell of the body. It passes through the other divisions of systemic circulation, making deliveries of oxygen and food to the capillaries. One local route is called *coronary* circulation, by which the heart receives its own supply of oxygen and food. The hard-working heart consumes about 10 times the nourishment needed by other organs and tissues, and it has its very own network of coronary arteries, veins, and capillaries.

After giving up its oxygen, blood turns from bright red to a dark purplish color. It passes from the capillaries to the smallest return vessels. From these venules, blood passes to the larger veins until it reaches the venae cavae. Blood from the head and arms returns to the heart through the superior vena cava, while the inferior vena cava brings blood from the lower parts of the body. Blood is sent from these largest veins back into the right atrium, where the story of this journey began, and the process starts all over again.

•　　　•　　　•　　　•

CHAPTER 4

. . . .

UNDERSTANDING THE BLOOD

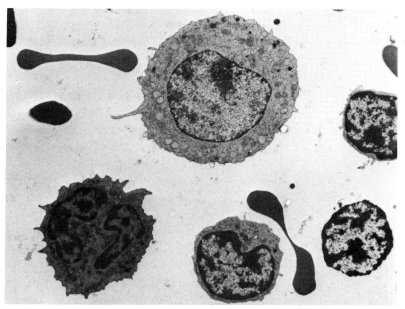

Human blood cells magnified 36,000x

Inside the vessels of the circulatory system, the body's only fluid tissue travels up to 10 miles every hour along its repeating course. This river of life that we know as the blood bathes every cell in the body in 20 seconds. When the body is at rest, it takes only 6 seconds for blood to go from the heart to the lungs and back; only 8 seconds for it to go to the brain and back; and only 16 seconds for blood to reach the toes and travel all the way back to the heart.

Blood is very different from other body tissue. Aside from being fluid, blood is the only tissue that is made up of cells that do not adhere to one another. All other human cells, such as nerve cells, muscle cells, and skin cells, join together in order to work together as tissue. Blood tissue, on the other hand, is made up of separated, specialized cells that are suspended in a living liquid.

There are between five and seven quarts of blood in the average adult man and one quart less in the average woman. The loss of more than two pints of blood is very dangerous. At such a point, just as in a water pipe with a leak, there is not enough force to keep the remaining blood in motion. If moving blood does not keep the blood vessels full, small vessels begin to collapse, circulation stops, and the rest of the blood becomes useless. If the blood cannot do its job, body cells begin to die very quickly. Brain cells are the first to die, living only for a few minutes without regular deliveries of oxygen by the blood cells.

Whole blood is made up of four basic parts. About 55% is a clear yellowish liquid called plasma. The solid part of the blood is made up of red bloods cells, white blood cells, and platelets. In .4 cubic inches of human blood (about the size of the head of

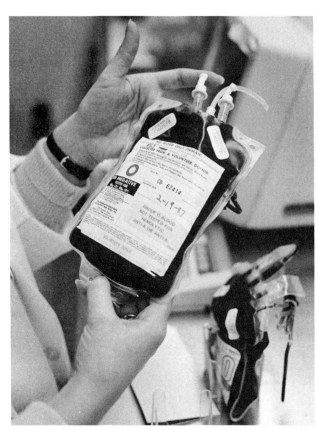

A unit of whole blood. Whole blood is made up of four basic parts. About 55% is a clear yellowish liquid called plasma; the solid part of blood contains red blood cells, white blood cells, and platelets.

a small pin) there are about 5,500,000 red cells; 4,000 to 10,000 white cells; and 250,000 to 500,000 platelets. Each part of the blood has its own special job to do. As working body tissue, the blood performs five important functions in the body. It carries vital materials such as digested food and oxygen to the cells; transports waste to parts of the body from where it can be released; carries chemical messengers between cells that are far from one another; fights disease and rebuilds damaged body tissue; and regulates the temperature of the body and helps to keep it warm.

PLASMA

Nearly one and a half gallons of blood plasma course through the blood vessels of an average adult. This warm straw-colored liquid is itself 92% water. The remaining 8% of plasma is composed of a variety of vital substances. Among them are dissolved *nutrients* such as glucose, fatty acids, amino acids, vitamins, and minerals. Nutrients are essential to the functioning of all bodily cells. Also present in plasma are special *proteins* such as fibrinogen, which helps the blood to clot, and various globulins. Plasma proteins help keep water inside the blood vessels and help to maintain normal blood pressure. *Antibodies,* which are important defensive proteins, are also in plasma. The ways in which antibodies help fight off bacteria and other unwelcome intruders in the body are discussed later in this chapter.

Plasma also contains a host of *hormones,* which are chemicals that are produced by the endocrine system and that regulate different activities in the body. One of these hormones is *secretin,* which is made in the lining of the small intestine. Its job is to begin the flow of the body's digestive juices. Insulin is another hormone found in plasma. This vital chemical is manufactured in the pancreas and is used by the body to burn its foremost energy fuel, glucose. Other important hormones are adrenaline, which speeds up the heart rate during an emergency, and thyroxine, which helps the cell burn food.

Glucose is a simple sugar that travels in the blood at a ratio of 1 part glucose to 1,000 parts blood. Circulating plasma delivers this vital energy nutrient to the cells. Excess glucose is converted to glycogen and stored in the liver and muscles for use as needed.

The proportion of salt in the plasma is 9 parts to 1,000. After delivery to the cells, plasma drops off excess salt at the kidneys. These organs are able to wash out both excess salt and a sudden overload of sugar. Through its circulatory pathways, plasma ensures the body of a proper balance of these nutrients.

Blood plasma carries extra water and urea, a protein waste, from the cells to the body's sweat glands and kidneys, where they can be released. Heat is also carried by blood plasma. During activity, plasma can take up heat from the muscles. As it flows through blood vessels near the skin, the plasma is cooled by the air. Because of its water content, plasma heats and cools slowly. As it circulates, plasma helps keep body tissues from overheating in much the same way as circulating water in a car radiator keeps the engine from overheating.

Plasma, therefore, plays a crucial role in maintaining the body's chemical balance, keeping its water content at a safe level, and regulating the body's temperature. At the same time, it serves as a fluid in which to suspend the other blood cells and transport oxygen and wastes. Doctors are able to fraction, or isolate, plasma so that it may be transfused to patients who need it. Doctors are also able to extract and use different parts of plasma for special conditions.

Remember that blood vessels must be kept full. Sometimes the body loses blood when no whole blood is available—on the battlefield, for example, or in a major car accident—or when there is no time to type the blood. In a condition known as circulatory shock, plasma leaks into the spaces between the cells. When such things happen, the fluid part of the blood must be replaced as soon as possible. During the 18th and 19th centuries solutions of water and salt, and even milk, were transfused into the body to restore fluid. Today, plasma can be separated from the blood cells and safely stored for long periods of time. It can be dried so that the water is evaporated while necessary proteins remain preserved. The plasma can then be frozen in sealed packets for easy storage and delivery. Its usefulness in fighting shock has made plasma a major treatment for wartime battle wounds.

During the 1940s, a Harvard research group headed by Edwin J. Cohn, M.D., developed ways to separate and purify certain plasma proteins. *Albumin* in plasma prevents uncontrolled bleeding. *Gamma globulin* can transfer temporary immunity to some diseases (such as measles and certain kinds of hepatitis) from the donor to the person receiving it. These and other fractions of plasma can also be frozen or powdered and stored for later use. Dr. Cohn also developed a method of taking only plasma from a blood donor. Because the body replaces plasma faster than it replaces whole blood, donors can give plasma five times more often with no harmful effects.

Afloat in the plasma are the trillions of blood cells that keep people alive and healthy. Most abundant in plasma are the oxygen carriers that give blood its red color: the red blood cells.

RED BLOOD CELLS

The 25 trillion red blood cells—or *erythrocytes*—in the human body make up almost 45% of the solid part of the blood. With a count of 5,500,000 cells per cubic inch of human blood, red blood cells outnumber white blood cells 1,000 to 1.

One-third of the red cell is *hemoglobin*, a protein compound that contains iron as well as the pigment that gives blood its red color. The primary job of red cells is to pick up oxygen at the lungs for delivery to the cells. At the lungs, these cells also carry away carbon dioxide, a byproduct of cell oxidation, or food burning. Hemoglobin in a red cell can pick up more than half of its own weight in oxygen, allowing red cells to transport 56,000,000,000,000,000,000,000,000 (56 septillion) atoms of oxygen a minute.

Hemoglobin molecules hook into oxygen molecules at capillaries in the lungs. Here, they drop off carbon dioxide molecules that attach to the hemoglobin when oxygen is released at the cells. Hemoglobin holds its passenger molecules loosely, so the changeover at the cells and lungs is very even. Oxygen-hungry blood turns purplish and returns to the heart for another trip to the lungs. This is why returning blood in the veins is not red. When bleeding from a vein occurs, oxygen in the air combines with hemoglobin to make the blood appear bright red again. Some types of animals really do have blue blood. Spineless animals such as crabs, lobsters, and snails use a compound of blue pigment and copper to pick up oxygen. Some sea worms have blood that is a green color, and one rare sea worm, the serpula, has blood that is both red and green.

Red blood cells are the only body cells that have no nucleus, or control center. Cells normally reproduce when the nucleus elongates and directs the cell to divide in two. With no nucleus, red cells cannot reproduce. Instead they have their beginnings in the hollows at the ends of bones. These hollows con-

Figure 4: The Pathway of an Oxygen Molecule. Oxygen diffuses from the alveolar membrane into the capillaries, where it is picked up by a hemoglobin molecule, transported to a group of cells, and released.

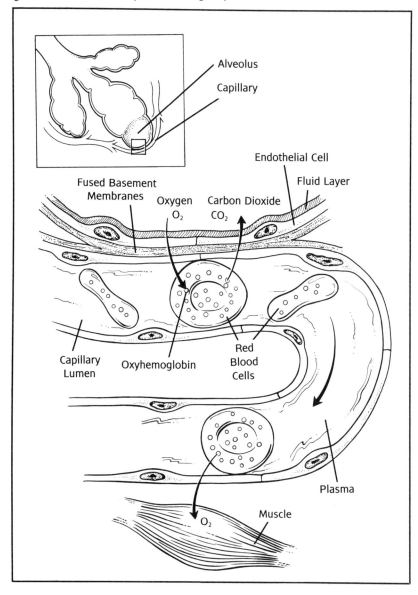

tain *marrow,* a mixture of blood and fat cells. Red marrow is found in skull and rib bones and at the ends of long bones of the arms and legs.

When red blood cells are first produced in the marrow, they are about $9/10,000$ of an inch in diameter, and they do have a nucleus. As the cells mature, the nuclei disappear, and after seven days, the grown cells leave the marrow to enter the mainstream of circulating blood. Red blood cells cannot move on their own; they are swept along by the flow of blood in the vessels. Often, they pile up against one another like a stack of plates. These piles of red blood cells go single file through microscopic blood vessels. All body cells border on these tubes. This is where all exchanges of material take place.

Because red blood cells wear out so quickly (10 million expire every second), 200 billion new cells must be formed every day, and the body's entire supply of red blood cells is completely renewed every four months. The average red cell lives for about four months. At this point the cells shrink to a third of their original size. As they circulate, the cells are jostled within the blood vessels and eventually break up into even smaller particles in the liver and the spleen.

The spleen is a small organ on the left side of the abdomen, below the stomach. It is thought of as the cemetery for red blood cells: a place where fragments of these cells are surrounded and destroyed. Any cells not destroyed in the spleen are finished off by the liver. The liver is able to change the red pigment in hemoglobin to green bile, a chemical that aids in fat digestion. The liver stores the iron from hemoglobin until it is carried by the blood to the red marrow in bones. Here, the iron will be used, along with materials salvaged from old cells by the spleen, to make new red blood cells.

WHITE BLOOD CELLS

White blood cells—or *leukocytes*—protect the body against infectious disease. These colorless cells, which are larger than most red blood cells, have no fixed shape. Most leukocytes move much like amoebas—microscopic one-celled Protozoa—by sticking out one part of their body and dragging the rest of themselves along. They can travel on their own and move against the current of the bloodstream. White blood cells can squeeze through the walls of capillaries and enter other tissues that are under attack from hostile organisms. It is their job to protect the body by destroying harmful germs. They remove the debris of outworn and displaced tissue cells, and they also rebuild and replace diseased or damaged body tissue.

White blood cells have a nucleus, but like red blood cells they do not reproduce by cell division. Most white blood cells are manufactured in the red marrow of the bones. Other leukocytes, which will be discussed later in this chapter, are formed in special glands elsewhere in the body. The red marrow and these glands can increase their output of white blood cells whenever the body is in danger. They are able to call up reserves of white blood cells, the body's soldiers, to fight off infection.

There are between 7 and 10 million leukocytes in every healthy cubic inch of blood. In the presence of infection, the body automatically produces a greater number of white corpuscles, or blood cells. A doctor can discover this increase by placing a blood sample on a special glass slide known as a *counting chamber*. The counting chamber has 400 tiny squares marked off on it. By counting the number of white blood cells in one square, it is easy to calculate the number of cells in a cubic inch or a cubic millimeter. A blood count that shows 20,000 or 30,000 white blood cells to the cubic millimeter tells the physician of a serious bacterial or viral invasion of the body.

In order to understand how leukocytes do their job, it is important to realize that there are 5 different kinds. Each kind has its own size, shape, and function. Three have small grains, or granules, in their body. These are the *neutrophils, acidophiles,* and *basophils. Lymphocytes* and *monocytes* do not contain granules. Granular leukocytes are formed in the red marrow. At first, they have no granules. As they mature, they go out into the bloodstream and acquire granules and a nucleus.

No one is certain about where nongranular monocytes are made. However, lymphocytes form in the *lymph glands* and *lymph nodes.* The lymphatic system is an independent network of tubing and fluid that hooks into the circulation system. One of its jobs is to act as a defense mechanism in the body. Lymphocytes participate in the manufacture of antibodies, which are proteins that help the body fight disease. Antibodies, as we saw earlier, are carried through the body in blood plasma. Some antibodies separate or clump invading bacteria. Others digest or kill them.

Antibodies also prepare bacteria for the action of germ-killing white blood cells. Those white corpuscles that engulf and devour germs are referred to as *phagocytes*.

Neutrophils are the most active of the phagocytes. They are able to surround and digest foreign matter such as splinters, dead or decaying cells, and harmful germs. These special white blood cells are attracted by chemicals given off by invading bacteria. They destroy bacteria in the bloodstream by pinning them against the walls of small capillaries, engulfing them and then digesting them. Remember that white blood cells can pass through capillaries to attack bacteria in other body tissues. Many neutrophils surround the part of the body that is healing and help to repair damage by changing to *scar-tissue* cells.

Whenever phagocytes engage in battle with infectious bacteria, some white corpuscles also become casualties. The thick yellow puss that forms during some infections is composed of dead body tissue, bacteria, and both dead and living white blood cells. The life span of leukocytes is about two weeks. As we have seen, some die fighting bacteria. Other leukocytes wander into the digestive tract or the kidneys and are lost with the body's excess water.

PLATELETS

As long as blood remains inside a blood vessel it flows freely. As soon as it leaves the vessel, it will flow for a while and then thicken and stop. It coagulates, or forms a *clot*, that plugs up the opening in the blood vessel. Without the formation of a clot, blood would continue to empty from the blood vessels just as water would leak out of a burst pipe. Coagulation of the blood is possible because of a microscopic, oval blood cell called a *platelet*, which resembles a tiny plate.

Platelets are fewer in number than red blood cells but greater in number than white blood cells. Roughly 300,000 platelets can be found in a cubic inch of human blood. These cells are very unusual because they adhere to anything they touch. Like white blood cells, platelets have a nucleus but do not reproduce themselves. They are manufactured in the red marrow of bone and in the lymph nodes, and they live in the body for about five days.

Platelets are most useful when they disintegrate. This happens when they are exposed to air, exposed to rough edges, shaken, or placed in contact with something nonliving (such as a bandage). This helps to explain why blood does not clot in the blood vessels yet begins to clot after it leaves an open cut.

When platelets touch the rough surface of a torn blood vessel, they break apart. A blood clot occurs when a thread-like substance called *fibrin* forms and entangles red cells and platelets. The clot hardens into a scab and covers the break. Fibrin is formed from a liver secretion, *fibrinogen*, which is a protein found in blood plasma. Fibrinogen is helped by a special chemical, *thrombin*, that is released into the blood by damaged platelets.

After a broken vessel is healed, the clot detaches and dissolves in the blood. Sometimes a clot can break loose and begin to travel in the bloodstream. Such a plug inside living tissue is called a *thrombus*. It is very dangerous. A thrombus can become lodged in a blood vessel that brings blood to the brain and cause one type of stroke. If a thrombus clogs a coronary artery, a heart attack may follow.

BLOOD TYPES

Even though all blood is made of plasma, red blood cells, white blood cells, and platelets, the blood of all people is not the same. There are four main blood types, or groups, into which all human blood can be placed. The type of blood a person has does not have anything to do with background or ancestry. Although blood is inherited from both parents, children in the same family may have different types of blood.

Blood of certain types cannot be given safely to people of certain other types. Before anyone can be given a blood transfusion, doctors must type the blood to find out to which blood group the patient belongs. If the wrong blood is given to someone, it is very dangerous. The person may become very ill or even die. This happens because chemicals in the red corpuscles of one blood type may be incompatible with the chemicals in the plasma of the other type. The blood plasma of one group will clump and destroy the red cells of an incompatible group. Therefore, it is essential that the blood of the donor be compatible with the blood of the recipient.

Most people have blood that belongs to one of the four main blood groups: A, B, AB, or O. All people may give or receive blood from their own group. People with type-O blood can give to any group. They are known as *universal donors*. Red cells in type-O blood will not be clumped by any other blood plasma. However, type-O people may receive blood only from other O- donors. People with type-AB blood can receive blood from any of the four groups. Plasma in AB blood does not contain chemicals that will clot any other red cells. Group-AB blood is called the *universal recipient*. However, AB blood may not be given to any group other than itself.

People with types A and B can receive blood from their own group or from the universal donor, type O. They can give blood to their own type or to type AB, the universal recipient. Even though it is possible to give and receive blood from other compatible groups, doctors have found that it is safest to give people blood from their own group.

High school students donate blood. Today, blood is tested for viral infections such as AIDS and hepatitis before it is banked or stored.

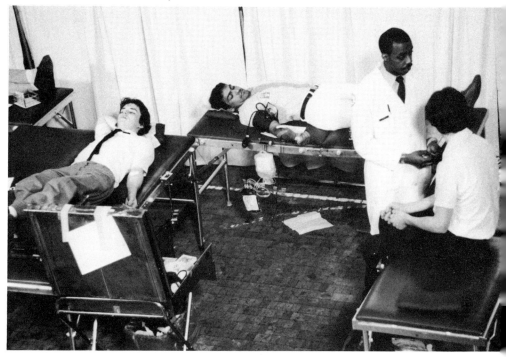

About 85% of human blood contains another important protein: the *Rh*, or *rhesus factor* (named after the rhesus monkey, in which it was first found). People who have this protein are Rh-positive (Rh +). Those who are Rh-negative (Rh −) lack this factor in their blood.

When an Rh − person receives blood from an Rh + person, white cells in the Rh − blood produce antibodies to fight the foreign proteins that have entered the body. In the process, they may destroy the red cells in the recipient's blood.

This becomes a serious problem if an Rh + man marries an Rh − negative woman. Because blood type is inherited, this couple may have an Rh + baby. If blood from the baby enters the mother's blood vessels, her white cells will develop antibodies against the Rh + proteins. If the woman has a second baby, the mother's antibodies may pass into the blood of the baby and destroy its red blood cells. In the past, Rh babies were often transfused at birth to replace the blood that carried the destructive antibodies. Today the mother can be given a vaccine that works against Rh disease.

A magnification of an occluded artery. Clots in the vessels that supply blood to the heart can result in heart attack and death.

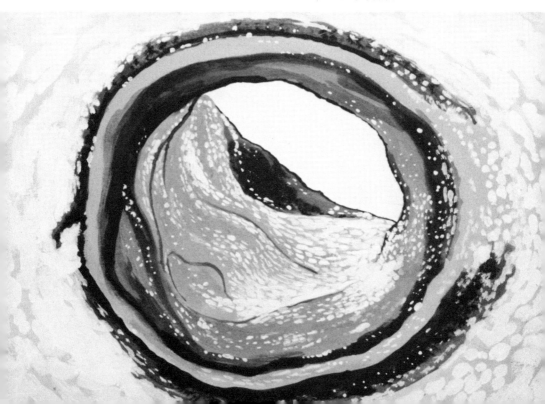

Blood can be donated at local hospitals, Red Cross centers, and private blood banks to be stored for later use. Blood banks can store whole and fragmented blood for more than a year. Today, donors at most centers are screened to make sure they are healthy enough to give blood. Most blood is tested for serious viral diseases such as hepatitis and AIDS before it is accepted for banking. All whole blood is typed when it is donated, to make certain that people in need of transfusions receive compatible blood. It is a good idea to ask your doctor to inform you about your own blood type. Because blood type never changes throughout a person's life, knowing what type of blood you need might save valuable time in an emergency.

BLOOD DISORDERS

Just as with other parts of the body, things can go wrong with the blood. Earlier in this chapter we discussed the dangers of floating blood clots. Blood clots may cause strokes or heart attacks or simply result in discomfort such as tingling and numbness in the fingers or toes. Blood clots in the veins may prevent blood from passing through. Blocked blood will back up into other tissues and cause swelling and possible tissue destruction. Such tissue congestion is called *hyperemia*.

A blood clot that is attached to the wall of a blood vessel is known as a *thrombus*. Such a clot decreases the amount of blood that is passing around it and may cause damage to tissues that are supposed to receive that blood. Tissue damage of this sort may lead to heart attacks, strokes, or kidney disease.

Thrombosis is a condition in which a blood clot forms in a blood vessel in the coronary artery. Another name for the kind of heart attack caused by this condition is *coronary thrombosis*. Today, medications such as dicumarol and other anticoagulants can be given to persons who are susceptible to heart attacks because clots in their circulatory system clog arteries that supply blood to the heart.

Thrombophlebitis can set in if a blood clot blocks a vein and the wall of the vein becomes inflamed. Thrombophlebitis of the deep leg or pelvis veins often occurs after someone has had surgery or a major illness that has kept them bedridden for a long period of time.

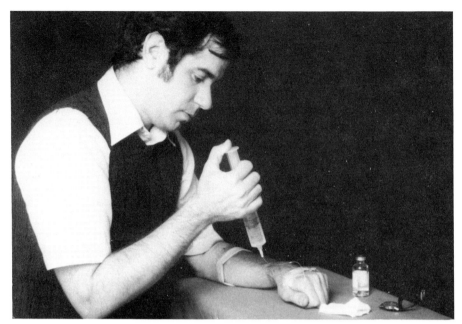

A hemophiliac injects himself with antihemophilic factor, an artificial clotting agent. The goal of this treatment is to keep clotting factor levels high enough to prevent internal bleeding episodes.

A blood clot that detaches and circulates in the bloodstream is called an *embolus*. An embolus may become trapped in a capillary and prevent blood from passing through. An *embolism* is a condition that results when an embolus clogs. An embolus in a vein leading to the lungs can cause a potentially fatal pulmonary embolism. When this occurs, some or all of the lung can be destroyed because it is unable to receive enough blood to keep its cells alive.

Serious conditions can result from the formation of blood clots that go astray. On the other hand, in a rare disease called *hemophilia*, blood does not clot quickly enough. Hemophilia is a condition that is passed by a mother to male children. (It is rarely found in females.) The platelets of hemophiliacs (patients afflicted with this disease) do not break up easily when their blood vessels are injured. When someone with hemophilia begins to bleed, there is no way to plug the opening in the vessel. Bleeding is excessive, and, without treatment or transfusions, it can be fatal. In some types of hemophilia, the body lacks the proteins needed to form fibrin. In recent years, hemophiliacs have been treated with an artificial clotting factor, which helps their blood to form lifesaving blood clots.

There are a number of other blood conditions that affect the body. In one blood disorder, *anemia,* the body does not have an adequate supply of red blood cells. In an anemic person, the number of red corpuscles per cubic millimeter may drop from 5 or 6 million to 2 million. This happens for a number of reasons: The red bone marrow may be unable to produce enough red blood cells, or it may produce imperfect ones. The spleen may destroy the red cells faster than they are being produced. Both of these conditions may take place at the same time.

There are several major types of anemia. One of the most common types is caused by a lack of iron. Iron-deficiency anemia may result from the long-term loss of blood or from diseases that deplete the body of iron.

Pernicious anemia occurs in people whose body lacks an important substance that transports Vitamin B_{12} to the bloodstream. Vitamin B_{12} is used in the formation of red blood cells. *Hemolytic anemia* is caused by an excessive destruction of red blood cells. In hemolytic anemia, red blood cells do not live out their full 120-day life span. Even though the cells die before their time,

The blood of a sickle-cell anemia victim. In this disorder, an inherited condition usually found in black people, abnormally shaped red blood cells are unable to transport enough oxygen to other body cells.

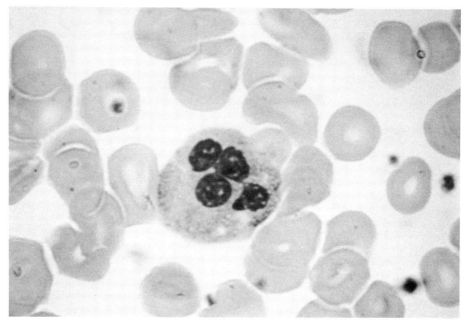

the marrow does not increase the output of red cells to make up for the loss. *Sickle-cell anemia* is an inherited condition usually found in black people. The name of this disorder comes from the unusual shape taken by the red blood cells. These abnormal cells are not able to carry enough oxygen to the body cells.

Leukemia is a general term that describes a number of types of cancer of the white blood cells. In this disorder, the red marrow or the lymph glands become diseased and overproduce white cells. The body becomes flooded with white blood cells that literally crowd out the other cells. Because it is so busy producing leukocytes, the body of a leukemia patient does not produce enough red blood cells, thus severe anemia results. The life of someone with leukemia can now be prolonged by transfusing red marrow from a donor into the patient. Recently, a National Bone Marrow Donor Registry was established to help leukemia patients find bone-marrow donors whose body tissue matches theirs. Advances such as this, as well as the ongoing research into blood disorders, is giving hope to thousands of people whose life depends on healthy, properly functioning blood.

•   •   •   •

CHAPTER 5

. . . .

COMMON HEART PROBLEMS

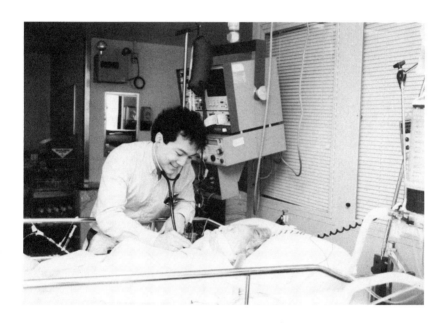

In the 20th century, and particularly since the mid-1960s, great progress has been made in understanding and correcting disorders of the circulatory system. Diseases that once would have caused severe disability or death can now be treated and often cured. Modern technology and surgical techniques can often can prolong the lives of people who are born with or who acquire heart disease. Yet, heart disease remains the nation's number-one killer. It is the leading cause of death in men from the age of 39 and in women from the age of 66.

Congenital Heart Defects

A congenital defect is one with which a person is born. One in every 100 babies is born with some congenital disorder of the heart. Some of these disorders are not at all serious and do not interfere with the child's normal, healthy development. Some heart defects become more life-threatening as the person matures, whereas others are so serious that immediate correction is needed to save the baby's life.

Congenital heart defects can be inherited. They are passed to the child from the parent or from a more distant grandparent, having skipped one or more generations before appearing in a newborn baby. Other disorders are the result of an infection or other physical upset in the mother. Exposure of a pregnant woman to an infection such as rubella (German measles) can affect her baby's heart. It is known that cigarettes, alcohol, and drugs can have serious negative effects on a developing fetus. Even a short-term reduction in oxygen, which might occur from flying in an unpressurized airplane, may threaten the proper development of a baby's heart.

The most common congenital disorder is a hole in the heart of a new baby. In a condition called a *ventricular septal defect*, there is a hole in the wall between the two ventricles. This allows oxygenated blood from the left side of the heart to be shunted to the right side. There, it mixes with the deoxygenated blood that travels to the pulmonary artery. Sometimes the septal opening is quite small and will close up by itself within the first two years of life. Other times it must be surgically sealed.

A hole can exist between the upper chambers as well. In *atrial septum defects*, blood from the left atrium flows to the right atrium. Pressure in the left heart is greater than in the right heart. As a result, the shunted blood goes on to the right ventricle and then to the lungs, overfilling and overburdening both the heart and pulmonary circulation.

In some congenital defects there are obstructions in the heart that prevent the free flow of blood. These often can be serious and must be corrected as soon as possible. There are three major causes of such blockages. First, the pulmonary, aortic, or tricuspid valves can be blocked, or *stenosed*, because their cusps are fused together and will not open properly. Second, a part of the

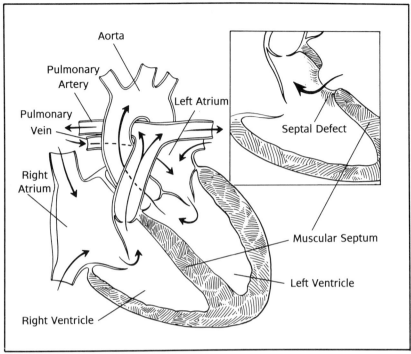

Figure 5: Ventricular Septal Defect. This diagram shows the normal flow of blood through the heart, highlighting the septal defect that allows the abnormal flow of blood from the left side of the heart to the right.

heart may be underdeveloped because of a decreased flow of blood to the heart. Third, there may be an overgrowth of muscle tissue in the heart.

Congenital obstructions can be outside the heart as well. Before birth, a baby does not use his or her lungs. In the fetus, an open vessel connects the aorta and pulmonary artery. Blood from the right side of the unborn baby's heart goes into the aorta instead of traveling to the lungs. Normally this vessel, the *ductus arteriosus,* closes up shortly after birth. In *patent ductus arteriosus,* it remains open, and there is another left-to-right shunt. The aorta will push blood into the pulmonary artery, where it mixes with deoxygenated blood going to the lungs. The open vessel must be quickly closed.

In another congenital condition, there is a narrowing of a part of the aorta. In this *coarctation* of the aorta, blood flows slowly in the narrowed region because the left ventricle has to work very hard to push blood past the pinched area. Because the extra effort demanded of the pumping chamber may lead to heart failure, the narrowing in the aorta must be surgically corrected. Fortunately, surgical treatment of congenital defects has become one of the most successful of all operations. Doctors can also diagnose many congenital disorders before birth. Ultrasound, which will be discussed further in this chapter, is a valuable instrument for the early detection of heart problems.

Infectious Diseases of the Heart

Infections that begin in any part of the body will reach the heart at some point. Normally, they pass through and cause no problems. However, if an invading organism finds a place in the heart in which to settle and grow, the heart itself begins to harbor an infectious disease. Infectious bacteria may come to rest in a part of the heart that has been misshapen because of a congenital condition or an acquired disease. Most susceptible to bacterial

Surgical replacement of the mitral valve. Infectious bacteria can cause permanent damage to the mitral valve; unfortunately, replacement valves can also become the targets of infection.

growths are the valves, holes in the heart, or an open ductus arteriosus.

Until recently, *rheumatic fever*, a condition involving inflammation of the joints and fever that can also affect the heart, was the most common cause of valve damage in the heart. Rheumatic fever is not itself an infection but rather a complication arising from a throat infection caused by a streptococcus bacteria. In order to fight the invading germ, the body's own immune system goes into action, but it may also act against body tissue. The heart is often the main target of this *autoimmune* reaction, which may also attack the lungs, the skin, and the nervous system. Fortunately, penicillin and other antibiotics are now used to treat streptococcus infections before the heart is affected.

A serious case of rheumatic fever may result in *myocarditis*, which is an inflammation of the heart muscle and the mitral and aortic valves. Complications that accompany this condition may lead to permanent damage to one or more heart valves. The valve damage occurs as years pass and scar tissue forms in these vital heart structures.

Infective endocarditis is a disease in which clumps of bacteria grow in a mitral valve. This condition can be caused by infections from other body parts that are carried to the heart by the blood. Intravenous drug users can develop endocarditis by injecting themselves with a dirty needle. The infectious bacteria can cause such severe damage to the mitral valve that the valve must be replaced. Unfortunately, replacement valves also become the targets of infection.

Patients can prevent endocarditis by taking antibiotics before infections have a chance to set in. For example, before having any dental work done they can take preventive antibiotics to kill germs from the mouth that can enter the bloodstream. A further complication of this disease occurs when pieces of infectious bacterial growth break off from the mitral valve and begin to travel in the arteries. This can cause serious problems in other parts of the body. For example, a bacterial fragment may get stuck in a vital organ such as the brain and cause death.

Pericarditis, an inflammation of the pericardium, may be caused by a number of things, including body infection. This damage to the sac that surrounds the heart is also caused by the body's autoimmune process. It may follow diseases such as rheumatic fever and certain forms of arthritis.

Pericarditis causes a pain in the chest that can be felt most strongly when taking a deep breath. A doctor will hear a rubbing sound when the heart beats. This is the sound of the two layers of the pericardium scraping against each other. There is no specific treatment for pericarditis, and it usually clears up by itself.

Sometimes, however, complications set in. The inflammation or tissue damage can destroy the space between the two layers. After a while the tissue may be replaced by a tight layer of scar tissue surrounding the heart. The scar tissue causes a condition called *constrictive pericarditis*. When this occurs, the scarred pericardium has to be removed by surgery. Fortunately, the heart can still work without a pericardium.

If the layers of the pericardium are not destroyed, another complication may set in. Blood or other fluid may accumulate between the two layers and form a *pericardial effusion*. If a large amount of fluid builds up, it will press inward against the heart, making it difficult for the heart to fill up completely. An effusion of this sort is a medical emergency. Doctors have to draw out the excess fluid from between the two layers of the pericardium so that the heart may beat freely again.

Acquired Heart Disease

Allen W. is 42 years old. Three months ago he returned home to find the elevator in his apartment building out of order. Feeling energetic, he bounded up the four flights of steps with little difficulty. But as he reached the final landing, Allen had a sudden, unpleasant feeling in his chest. It was not really a pain but rather a heaviness, a slight pressure under his breastbone. "I'm not as young as I used to be," he thought to himself. Once in his apartment, Allen sat down for a few minutes' rest and the discomfort went away.

As the weeks went by, Allen had a number of similar experiences. After a game of tennis he would become a bit more breathless than usual, and the tightness in his chest stayed a few minutes longer. Still, he would feel fine again after a brief rest and was certain that he was simply out of shape. Last week Allen had another chest pain. This time the pain gripped his chest more severely. It spread to his neck and jaw. He began to perspire and felt faint and nauseous. This time, he could not blame the symptoms on too much activity. This time, Allen was having a heart attack.

The initial chest pains that Allen experienced were the first symptoms of *coronary artery disease* (CAD). Allen's heart muscle was not receiving enough oxygen to do its job because something was blocking one of his coronary arteries. While he was at rest, enough blood was getting through the artery. With extra activity, however, Allen's heart had to work harder to supply itself with extra oxygen. Because of the blockage, the heart muscle was unable to get the needed oxygen, which caused a chest discomfort called *angina pectoris*. This is the pain that Allen first experienced, and it should have served as a warning to him that he should ease the work load on his heart.   Thousands of men and women feel the early warning signals of CAD every day. Their coronary arteries become blocked with hard deposits of fat and other cell accumulations called plaque. At first, when the buildup is rather slight, blood is able to pass right over it. But as the plaque increases and as more material builds up, the blood can hardly pass by. Eventually the artery may become completely blocked, and blood is unable to reach the heart to deliver its precious cargo.

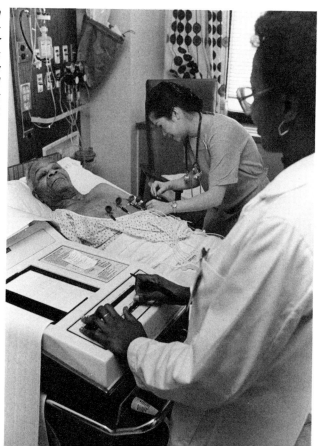

A hospital technician administers an electrocardiograph to her patient. This test records the electrical activity of the heart and is used to diagnose heart attacks and other cardiac malfunctions.

The process of plaque buildup is called *atherosclerosis*. As the condition develops, the inner lining of the artery wall deteriorates. Atherosclerosis accounts for 99% of all cases of CAD. Plaque can build up in any blood vessel in the body, but it is most dangerous when it accumulates in the coronary arteries. Buildup in these vessels slows down or stops blood that is flowing to the heart. The heart needs a good blood supply from the coronary arteries. Without sufficient oxygen to fuel the heart's strenuous work, heart cells begin to die and serious consequences follow.

Material that can block blood vessels builds over a long period of time. Plaque in the coronary arteries may not show its deadly nature for many years. It begins forming early in a person's life and reaches an advanced stage when that person reaches middle age. The dangerous material that develops into plaque does its work gradually. Remember that the inner lining of a healthy artery is smooth and elastic. It is here that the first damage of atherosclerosis begins. In the earliest stage of this disease, yellow fatty streaks can be seen forming on the inner surface of the artery, usually in places where there is branching.

In the second stage, the deposits get thicker and harder. The smooth muscle cells from the wall of the artery begin to increase. They combine with fatty tissue to form white, irregular masses that grow out of the arterial wall. Platelets from the blood then become trapped in the plaque. Normally, people who are in these first two stages of atherosclerosis feel no symptoms of disease.

Next, the accumulation of materials (calcium, fibrous bone tissue, cholesterol, and clots) begins to clog the arteries. Little or no blood is able to get through the plaque that has narrowed the blood vessel, and body organs begin to suffer from ischemia, a lack of blood and oxygen. If the coronary arteries that lead to the heart are severely blocked, the part of the heart that is supposed to receive blood from that artery may die, even though the rest of the heart goes on working. More simply, the person has a heart attack.

The Heart Attack

When Allen W. experienced severe pain, he did not know what was wrong. He waited for the pain to subside, and when it did not, he thought that it might be a case of acute indigestion, a discomfort from something he had eaten. But when the pain

TO SAVE A LIFE

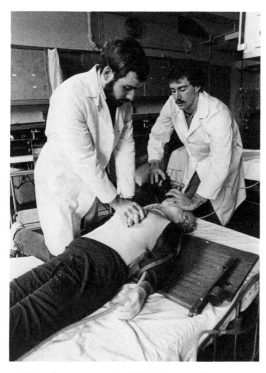

Doctors demonstrate cardiopulmonary resuscitation (CPR).

The first step in CPR is to tilt the victim's head back to provide a clear air passage past the tongue. The next step is to breathe into the victim's mouth in an effort to inflate the lungs. Cardiac compression involves manually depressing the lower breastbone strongly and rhythmically in order to force blood through the heart and lungs and out to the body. If there is only 1 rescuer on the scene, the chest is compressed 80 times per minute. After every 15 compressions, the rescuer will breathe 2 mouthfuls of air into the lungs. If 2 rescuers are present, the first compresses the chest at a steady rate of 60 per minute, and the second gives a breath after every 5th compression.

CPR is not a simple process, but it can easily be learned by most people. Among many other things, CPR training teaches the rescuer proper positioning of the body and how to locate the safe pressure spot for chest compression. The full-day training course given by the Red Cross teaches people to make crucial decisions during a life-and-death situation. The Red Cross then tests and certifies that people who pass CPR training are capable of administering this life-saving technique.

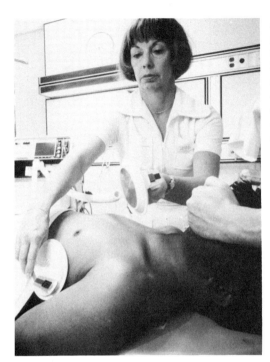

An emergency room nurse uses an enfibrillator on a heart attack victim. This device passes a short, sharp electric current through the heart of an attack victim and shocks it back into a regular rhythm.

spread, Allen wisely asked a friend to take him to the emergency room of a local hospital. There, after taking an electrocardiograph (see Chapter 6), the doctor was able to see the electrical activity of Allen's heart and diagnosed the problem very quickly. Allen's symptoms were caused by a *myocardial infarction*, a type of heart attack.

The narrowing or clogging of a coronary artery from a build-up of plaque may cause heart muscle to infarct, or die of oxygen deficiency. A myocardial infarction is one kind of serious heart attack. Damage to heart muscle may be quite mild or severe enough to cause death. Fortunately, many people who are treated promptly survive heart attacks. If someone does survive a myocardial infarction, he or she may have to deal with permanent damage to the heart because the area of the infarction becomes like scar tissue. It is still part of the heart's structure, but it no longer contracts properly or does the job it was intended to do.

Not every heart attack is an infarction. The term *heart attack* covers a range of disturbances in the heart's function. A coronary thrombosis, in which there is sudden blockage of a coronary artery, is a heart attack. But so is an unexplained disorder in the heart's rhythm. Some people even have silent heart attacks. They feel no pain and are unaware of any problem until other symptoms lead a doctor to suspect that there is heart damage.

A heart-attack patient is always kept in the coronary care unit of a hospital for several days and watched closely for any complications that may arise. One problem that doctors watch for is *congestive heart failure*, which occurs when the damaged area of the heart is unable to do its share of the work. For example, the ventricle may not be capable of pumping out as much blood as before. The patient may become short of breath and retain body fluids, because insufficient oxygen is reaching the lungs and kidneys. By using special medications, the doctor is often able to get rid of the excess fluid, open up blood vessels, and decrease the heart rate.

Another serious condition to watch for after an infarction is called an *aneurysm*. Here, the wall of the heart may balloon out or even burst open. A ballooning aneurysm can be treated surgically. If the aneurysm bursts, it is usually fatal. The dangers of complication decrease with time, and a recovering heart-attack patient is often judged to be out of danger. At this point a full program of rehabilitation is begun.

After hospital treatment, people who have had heart attacks often continue to take medication and rest at home. Doctors are usually able to determine what factors contributed to a heart attack. A surviving patient may be placed on a special diet or told to limit strenuous activity. In many cases, heart-attack patients can be helped by surgery, either immediately or at a later date. Encouragingly, many people who suffer heart attacks recover to live out a full and active life.

Cardiac Arrest

One out of every two heart attack victims will die in a few hours if no assistance is at hand. Most of these fatal attacks are sudden ones that come on without any warning and are caused by a *fibrillation* of the ventricles. During a fibrillation, the heart muscle does not contract rhythmically as one unit. Instead, it quivers rapidly, with no set pace, and soon degenerates into something resembling a bag of wriggling worms. The uncoordinated muscle tissues cannot pump blood around the body. If the fibrillation is not reversed, only minutes stand between their onset condition and *cardiac arrest*, in which the heart has come to a stop, and in which there is no beat, no pulse, and no blood pressure.

A hospital emergency room is usually equipped to handle cases of cardiac arrest. Doctors can pass a short, sharp electric current through the heart and shock it back into a regular rhythm. But too many people in cardiac arrest never reach a hospital. Remember that brain cells die in four minutes. Heart cells die in 10 minutes. When minutes count, even the time spent waiting for an emergency service ambulance or the fire department may be too long. The difference between life and death may lie in the hands of a bystander who has been trained in *cardiopulmonary resuscitation* (CPR). This method of first aid is a combination of mouth-to-mouth breathing, which supplies oxygen to the lungs, and chest compression, which circulates blood. People who are trained in CPR can save a life by restoring the beat of a heart that has stopped.

•   •   •   •

CHAPTER 6
· · · · · · · · · · · · · · · ·
TREATING HEART PROBLEMS

Drs. Christiaan Barnard, Adrian Kantorowicz, and Michael DeBakey

People who suffer from acquired heart disease are often convinced that their life will be permanently degraded. They worry about the things that they will no longer be allowed or be able to do, and they fear that little can be done to help someone with a damaged heart or circulatory system. Fortunately, advances in modern medicine and technology have given many heart patients new options.

Most people who experience discomfort visit their family doctor first. The family physician makes the initial diagnosis that a heart problem may exist. In many cases, he or she may want a second opinion from a specialist. A cardiologist, a doctor who specializes in treating disorders of the heart, has many sophisticated and effective instruments with which to work. Some of these tools help to diagnose the nature of a problem so that proper treatment can be planned.

The Physical Examination

A person who experiences any symptoms of heart disease should seek medical help as soon as possible. Most people would be surprised at how much a physician can learn about a patient during a routine physical examination. A doctor can determine many things about a patient's condition by simply using his or her senses of sight, hearing, and touch.

During the examination, the doctor may palpate, or feel, the heart. He or she often can detect irregularities from the way the heartbeats feel. By listening to the heart with a stethoscope, the doctor can hear unusual sounds that might be coming from the heart or lungs. The doctor listens for sounds that the blood makes as it moves through valves. The stethoscope also indicates how well the chambers are contracting and how normally the blood is circulating. The doctor then determines the rate of the heart by measuring the patient's pulse.

A coronary care unit nurse checks the blood pressure of a cardiac patient. Blood pressure readings can determine, among other things, the volume of the blood flow and the force of the heart's contractions.

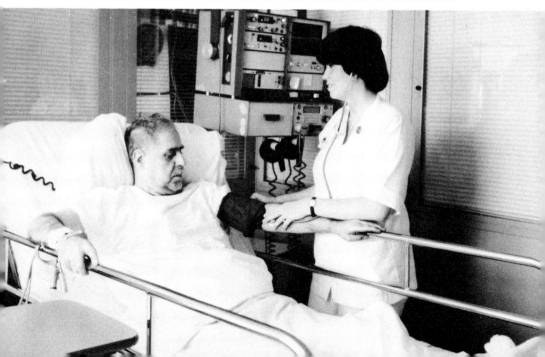

As it flows through the body, blood presses against the walls of the blood vessels. A routine blood-pressure reading is taken as part of every physical examination. This is done with a *sphygmomanometer*, a simple mercury pressure gauge attached to a cuff that fits around the upper arm. The cuff is inflated to block off the pulse at the elbow, and a stethoscope is placed over the main artery in the arm. Then the air in the cuff is released, and the blocked blood rushes ahead. The doctor listens for a sound of systolic (contracting) pressure as the blood rushes through, and notes the reading on the mercury dial of the "sphygmo." As the cuff is deflated again and the blood flows evenly, the doctor listens to the sound and observes the reading of diastolic (relaxation) pressure.

A blood-pressure reading can give the doctor vital information about the volume of the blood flow and the force of the heart's contractions. It can help the doctor determine the condition of elastic tissues in the arteries and how well the smaller arterioles are expanding and contracting. High blood pressure is a major cause of CAD. In Chapter 7, we will take a closer look at the dangers of high blood pressure.

The job of the heart is to deliver necessary materials to the rest of the body. Any disorder in the functioning of circulation may affect the health of other body organs. In order to find out how well the body's organs are working, the doctor may test samples of blood and urine during the examination. In some cases, the patient also may be given a straight X-ray. This will show the doctor whether any of the heart's chambers are enlarged. An X ray can also show abnormal heart rate or rhythm.

Every part of a routine examination supplies the physician with important diagnostic information about the patient's heart. Often, the family doctor is able to treat minor problems of the circulatory system. However, if a more serious heart problem is suspected, it may become necessary for a cardiologist to take a much closer look at the patient's heart.

Looking Inside the Heart

One of the most useful cardiological tools is the *electrocardiograph*, or EKG. This sensitive machine is able to measure very tiny changes in electrical currents. When the heart beats, there are slight changes in the current it sends through the heart mus-

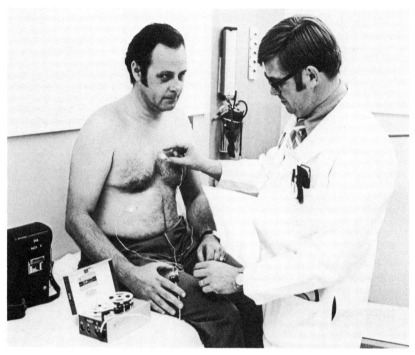

A doctor at Stanford University demonstrates the ambulatory EKG he developed in 1971. It recorded the heart's electrical activity for a 10-hour period; today's models can record a full day's heart activity.

cle. An EKG is able to detect and chart the size and direction of these tiny changes. It is able to show any disturbances in the heart's own pacemaker system.

When a person is given an EKG, three pairs of wires are attached in a special order to the patient's arms and legs. Several wires are also placed on the patient's chest. As the EKG picks up the electrical activity of the heart, it prints out a graph of tall and short peaks that represent the muscular contractions of the heart. By looking at the peaks, the low points, and the rhythms of the printout, a cardiologist can see subtle changes that another person might not even notice. The cardiologist is able to see the fingerprints of different kinds of heart disease. Abnormal patterns on the graph can show such irregularities as fluttering of the atria or fibrillation of any of the chambers. The EKG reading can show a block in the heart or damage to the heart wall. In effect, the EKG is able to show the presence of overworked, injured, or dead cardiac muscle.

An ordinary EKG is given in the doctor's office while the patient is lying down and relaxed. However, a cardiologist might want a record of the heart's electrical activity under specific conditions. A *stress EKG* is used to show how the heart responds to increased work. A patient might be wired to a stress EKG while riding a stationary bicycle or pacing on a treadmill. The EKG will print out its results as the patient pedals or walks more and more rapidly.

The doctor also might want to look for electrical disturbances that take place during a patient's normal daily activity. A lightweight miniature *ambulatory EKG* can be wired to someone and easily carried around at home or at work for a period of 24 hours or more. When recorded by an ambulatory EKG, a full day's heart activity can be reviewed by the cardiologist in about four minutes.

Another important diagnostic tool is the *cardiac catheter*. To use this instrument, the doctor inserts a long thin tube into a blood vessel in the patient's arm. Then, with the help of an X

A patient undergoes a heart stress test at a New York City hospital. A stress EKG records how the heart responds to increased work.

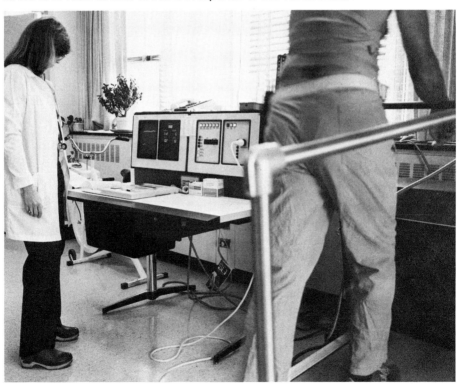

ray, the tube is gently pushed into the heart. The cardiac catheter can measure blood pressure in the heart chambers. It also can collect blood samples from different parts of the heart. In this way the doctor can determine how much oxygen is reaching the heart cells and discover any shunting (the passing of blood from one side of the heart to the other).

The doctor can explore the heart even more fully by injecting a dye through the catheter after it has reached the heart. A quick series of X rays can show how the dye moves through the patient's heart and blood vessels. These pictures, or *angiograms*, can give the doctor a clear view of blood vessels and heart chambers. They show any obstructions, enlargements, or damage in the area reached by the catheter.

It is also possible to inject radioactive materials (radioisotopes) into a patient's bloodstream. A scanner can follow the journey of the isotope as it flows to the heart. By actually entering the blood vessels, elements such as thallium-200 provide the doctor with still more information about a person's heart and circulation.

Another method of investigating the heart and blood vessels— one that is *noninvasive* (does not involve any entry into the body itself)—is *ultrasound echocardiography*. This is a very safe and accurate diagnostic tool for the cardiologist. It uses sound waves of very high frequency—much too high for the human ear to hear. These ultrasonic waves are similar to the sound waves bats use while moving through the air. When sound waves such as these bounce back to the bat, the echoes produced provide information about the position, shape, and movement of other objects. In the same way, ultrasonic waves are bounced off different parts of the heart from different positions. From the echoes that return, a picture can be built up of the shape and movement of the heart walls, chambers, and valves.

High-tech Treatments

In recent years, open-heart surgery has become a safe, reliable tool for relieving the effects of many heart problems. But such major surgery rarely is the first choice of treatment for a heart patient. Modern technology has also given the doctor other, less extreme ways to save and extend the lives of people with disorders of the heart and blood vessels.

One of these methods is *balloon angioplasty,* a technique used to treat a constriction of the coronary artery. A catheter with a tiny balloon in its tip is slipped through an artery to the constricted area. The balloon is inflated, pushing out the walls of the coronary artery and crushing the accumulated plaque. At the same moment, the balloon angioplasty can be viewed by the doctor on a television screen.

Each year, more than 30,000 people in the United States receive another kind of catheter treatment, the *balloon pump.* In this procedure, the catheter is inserted into an artery in the groin and gently pushed into the aorta. At the end of the catheter is a fine sausage-shaped balloon, about 25 centimeters long. Helium is rhythmically pumped in and out of the balloon. As it expands and contracts, the balloon helps the pumping action of the heart and improves the flow of blood to the body parts. The balloon pump is often allowed to remain in a patient for several months until he or she is ready for heart surgery.

An experimental technique that is still being tested involves the use of cool laser beams to clean clogged arteries. The light

Sharon Owens poses with a doctor in 1982 at Johns Hopkins Children's Center. Sharon was the first patient to be treated with balloon angioplasty, a technique used for correcting a blocked heart valve.

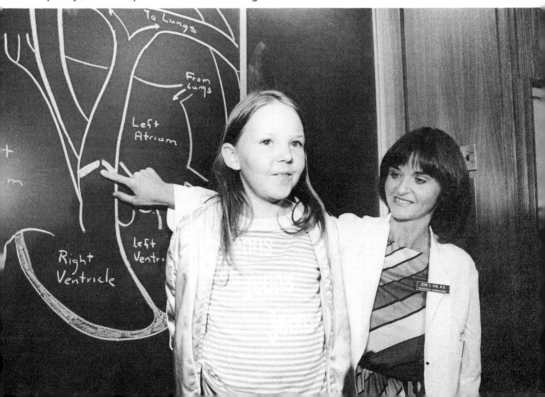

This compact pacemaker can be implanted in the chest to transmit impulses to the heart that keep it beating 70 times a minute.

of lasers is so concentrated that it can melt plaque like butter. By using *laser angioplasty,* the surgeon can thread a laser-tipped catheter through arm or leg arteries to clogged arteries. There, a laser beam is fired to burn away fatty deposits and clear the vessel. Perfecting this technique will be of enormous benefit. At present, an operation to bypass a clogged artery takes several hours. Laser cleaning takes only five minutes.

Chapter 3 described how the sinus node in the right atrium sends electrical signals along special conducting fibers to the septum and the ventricles. These signals direct the atria to contract, and ventricle contraction follows a fraction of a second later. When the heart contracts and relaxes at a regular rate, there is a smooth flow of blood through the chambers.

Sometimes, some or all of these impulses are blocked from reaching the lower half of the heart. A continuous heart block can permanently reduce the heart's action. The heart can slow down to a sluggish 30 beats per minute, a condition during which even the slightest exertion would cause a person to become very short of breath. An interruption of the heart's triggering mechanism can be corrected. Doctors can implant an artificial pacemaker into the chest. This lightweight, compact device is operated by long-lasting, rechargeable batteries. It can transmit impulses directly to the heart and keep it beating 70 times every minute. The pacemaker can send impulses either continuously or only when the heart's natural signal goes wrong.

Hundreds of thousands of people all over the world have pacemakers. There is no real danger that the pacemaker will malfunction or weaken. Sometimes the rate of an artificial pacemaker can be disrupted by metal detectors, microwaves, some electrical tools, or even certain hospital equipment. Many new pacemakers will shut off automatically if their impulses are interfered with. However, if anything does go wrong, the wearer can call a doctor to arrange for a fresh battery pack or a new pacemaker.

A recent improvement allows some pacemakers to function on demand. These can respond to changing physical needs as a person's activity varies. The pacemaker will adjust its signal so that the heart will beat faster with more exertion. Even greater improvements are in the planning stages. The pacemaker of the near future will be controlled by a computer. It will be able to monitor and store information about the wearer's heart rhythms. The computer will be able to transmit data to a cardiac center for instant printout. The doctor, in turn, will be able to adjust and regulate the pacemaker accurately without ever having to see the patient.

Heart Medications

Doctors have a wide range of medications with which to treat heart problems. There are more than 100 drugs that can be used alone or in combination with others to relieve the symptoms and stress of heart disease. Some of these medications have been in use for a long time, some have been introduced very recently, and some are still being studied for possible use in the future.

The oldest medical remedy in continual use is *digitalis*. This herbal extract has been used to make the heart pump more efficiently for more than 200 years. The active chemicals in digitalis medicines are called *cardiac glycosides*. They help the heart muscles pump more powerfully without using more oxygen. As a result, there is less back-flow pressure in the heart, less blood accumulating in the chambers, and a better blood flow to the kidneys.

Angina pains are caused by a problem in the coronary arteries, which supply blood to the heart. *Nitrites* and *nitrates* are drugs that dilate, or open up, the blood vessels so that blood can flow more freely and relieve the pain. The most common of these medications is known to most people as *nitroglycerin*, the same substance that is used to make dynamite. As a medicine, however, nitroglycerin comes in perfectly harmless half-milligram tablets.

Another treatment for angina uses one of a number of compounds that are known as *beta blockers*. One such common medication is *propranolol*. The heart's action is determined by the amount of physical activity it has to support and the amount of emotional stress that is put on it. Beta blockers shield or block extra stimulation (from exercise or emotions) from reaching special nerves in the body. If the heart is receiving a high level of stimulation, the beta blockers keep it from speeding up and needing more oxygen.

There are three major causes of blockages that can set off a heart attack: spasms in artery walls that squeeze off the blood supply; blood clots; and fatty deposits of plaque. *Channel blockers* are given in pill form to prevent arteries from contracting. Calcium is a mineral that takes part in the formation of plaque. Calcium channel blockers not only stop spasms but also keep calcium from entering the cells of the walls of coronary vessels. They also help to control the heart's rhythm and reduce blood pressure.

Anticoagulants are drugs that are designed to interfere with and sometimes prevent clotting. Some anticoagulants, such as heparin, are injected into the bloodstream. Others, such as nicoumalone and warfarin, are taken orally. Streptokinase, an enzyme, is a powerful anticoagulant that can cause a clot to dissolve in about an hour. It must be injected very soon after the onset of a heart attack. At present, this drug takes special skill to administer—it is given by a catheter that is snaked into a coronary artery—and is not yet available in all hospitals.

Tissue plasminogen activator (t-PA) is a new drug that was approved for use in the United States in November 1987. T-PA travels in the bloodstream until it meets a clot and then dissolves it without damaging the heart muscle in any way. This drug works best if it is administered within six hours of a heart attack. It offers new hope to heart patients because t-PA seems to limit the damage caused by a heart attack without affecting the normal clotting that takes place elsewhere in the body.

Controlling Cholesterol Levels

Cholesterol, a *lipoprotein* (a protein that dissolves in certain organic solvents), is produced by the body and found in food. There are good (high density) and bad (low density) cholesterols. Because abnormally high levels of cholesterol can contribute to atherosclerosis, doctors are placing high hopes on a number of drugs that can lower levels of harmful cholesterol. Among these drugs is *gemfibrozil,* which lowers the overall level of cholesterol slightly but changes the types of cholesterol in the blood in ways that reduce the risk of CAD.

Gemfibrozil has fewer side effects than cholesterol drugs such as *lovastatin,* which is able to lower cholesterol levels considerably. Because lovastatin is considered less safe to use than gemfibrozil, it is normally given to patients who have had previous heart attacks and/or who have very high cholesterol levels.

A dramatic study published in the January 28, 1988, issue of *The New England Journal of Medicine* by Charles H. Hennekens, M.D., of Harvard University, showed that ordinary aspirin can be used as an important preventive medicine in fighting heart disease. The five-year study showed that taking a single aspirin tablet every other day can sharply reduce the risk of having, or dying from, a heart attack. Aspirin cannot reverse damage that has already begun in the heart or blood vessels, but in people who are at low risk and who are otherwise healthy, it can reduce the chances of myocardial infarction by as much as 50%.

There are many other drugs that are helpful in the treatment of heart disorders. An inefficient heart can cause the kidneys to become impaired. *Diuretics* are used to help the kidneys increase the body's output of salts and water. A variety of other drugs can correct *arrhythmia,* a disruption the heart's natural rhythm. In addition to the more than 100 medications that are presently available, a number of promising experimental drugs are being studied and tested for future use. Today, drugs for the heart and blood vessels—when used under proper medical supervision—play a major role in easing distress and prolonging life.

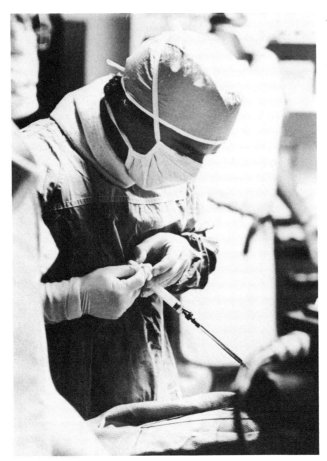

A doctor injects an anti-coagulant through a tiny tube into a heart attack patient to break up the blood clots that caused the attack.

Heart Surgery

Some circulatory problems can only be alleviated by surgery. Progress in open-heart surgery has made it possible for surgeons to sew up abnormal openings in the heart and rearrange the inside of a deformed heart. Modern surgical techniques can relieve some major acquired heart problems and, most remarkably, can replace the heart itself. The most common operations performed on heart patients are for acquired diseases of the coronary arteries and the valves. In the United States alone, more than 100,000 people undergo *coronary bypass* operations each year.

During this procedure—which was pioneered in the early 1960s by Dr. Michael De Bakey and Dr. Edward Garrett at Baylor College Medical Center in Houston, Texas—a nonessential healthy leg vein is grafted onto an obstructed artery, giving the blood an unblocked path through which to flow. In a coronary bypass, the graft passes directly from the aorta to an area beyond the obstruction in the coronary artery. By increasing the supply of blood to heart, the operation relieves uncontrollable angina pains. Multiple bypasses of several arteries can be made during the same operation. The use of the patient's own vein eliminates any possibility that the body will reject the new pathway.

An alternative to bypass grafting is an *endarterectomy*, in which the doctor attempts to remove obstructions in the artery. During this procedure the surgeon opens the artery and breaks away plaque from the artery wall with a blunt instrument or a fine spray of carbon dioxide gas.

The heart valves that are most likely to become diseased are the mitral (inlet) valve, and the aortic (outlet) valve, in either side of the left ventricle. Today, with improved artificial valves available, more and more defective valves are being replaced rather than repaired. (Surgery on an aortic valve is all but impossible.)

Mechanical valves are extremely durable, come in a variety of sizes, and are easy to sterilize. However, clots can form around the artificial materials used in making the valves. As a result, people with artificial valves have to take anticoagulants for the rest of their life. Many prefer to use biological valves, which are made from pig valves or calf pericardium or come from human donors. Biological valves are silent—in contrast to mechanical valves, which make a clicking noise—and do not require the use of anticoagulants, but they are not as durable as artificial valves.

Heart Transplantation

Aneurysms, described briefly in Chapter 5, occur when the wall of a blood vessel begins to swell up and protrude. This dangerous bulge, which also can occur in the aorta, can be removed by surgery. Heart tumors also can be removed in the operating room. Sometimes, however, the heart is so diseased that no repair work is possible. When this happens, the only way to save a patient's life may be a *heart transplant.*

Transplant surgery has come a long way since 1967, when Dr. Christiaan Barnard performed the first heart transplant in Capetown, South Africa. At that time the body's rejection of foreign tissue made the heart transplant a very risky procedure. In 1972, doctors developed the *biotome*, a device to monitor severe rejection reactions in transplant patients. By 1977, donor hearts could be transported over relatively long distances by airplane for the first time. In 1983, cyclosporine, the first antirejection drug, was approved for use in the United States. This drug is now used in combination with azathioprine and steroids to combat many rejection problems, turning transplant surgery into an almost routine operation.

Transplant surgery has raised a number of questions that have never before been raised. Many moral and ethical problems related to heart replacement are yet be to resolved. Doctors often have to make a choice of who will get the small number of donor hearts needed by so many critically ill patients. The medical community will have to face more conflicts over the use of animal organs, such as the baboon heart that kept Baby Fae alive for three weeks in Loma Linda, California, in 1984. There are many questions concerning a doctor's right to remove the heart from a donor who is not yet medically dead but who has suffered irreparable brain damage and can "survive" only on a life-sustaining machine.

Still, the treatments continue. Fortunately, only a fraction of people with heart disease require transplants, and only a minority of people with coronary blockage need surgery. The vast majority of heart patients can be treated effectively with drugs and can then lead a healthy life. And as people learn more about preventing the diseases that the heart can acquire, perhaps even the most effective treatment will become unnecessary.

•   •   •   •

CHAPTER 7

· · · · · · · · · · · · · ·

PREVENTING
HEART DISEASE

In 1948, the United States government began an ongoing study of the living habits, medical histories, and deaths of some 5,000 residents of a small town outside Boston, Massachusetts. The Framingham Heart Study, as it has come to be known, has provided a great deal of knowledge about the prevention of heart disease. Over the years, the study had found three major risk factors associated with heart disease: smoking, high blood pressure, and high levels of cholesterol in the blood. This chapter will examine these risk factors, as well as some of the other conditions that are in some way connected with an increase in the frequency of the nation's number-one killer.

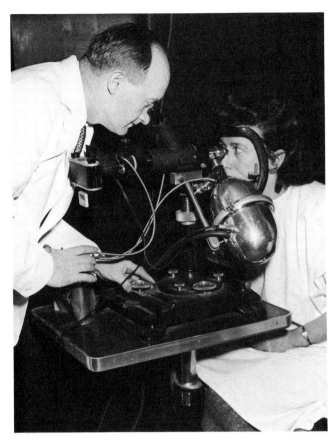

A 1952 photograph of a participant in the Framingham Heart Study. The doctor is taking a magnified picture of the arteries of her eye to determine changes in blood vessels associated with hypertension.

SMOKING AND HEART DISEASE

The Framingham Study named cigarette smoking as the number-one risk factor of heart disease. The facts are clear and devastating: Smoking is related to 30% of all deaths caused by coronary artery disease, and about half of the 35,000 deaths from smoking every year in the United States come from a heart attack.

Despite a decline in the past few years, there are still more than 50 million adult smokers in this country. Of these, the "light" (1 pack a day or less) smokers have a 70% greater risk of dying of heart attack than do nonsmokers, and 2 or more packs a day give the smoker a 200% greater risk. Smoking low-tar-and-nicotine brands of cigarettes does not lessen a smoker's chances of suffering the cardiovascular disease.

In tests performed on animals, cigarette smoke has been shown to cause fibrillation, the bag-of-worms movement of heart muscles described in Chapter 5. Fibrillation brings on the sudden-death heart attack, which is most common in men in their 30s and 40s, the age group most at risk of having some type of smoking-related heart attack. Other studies of smokers who have acquired heart disease clearly show how cigarette smoke damages the circulatory system.

Carbon monoxide is a chemical depressant in smoke that keeps red corpuscles from working properly. As a result, smoke starves the cardiac muscles of necessary oxygen. At the same time, the heart needs more oxygen because it is being stimulated by nicotine to beat faster. Smoke also raises blood pressure in the body. It can injure the cells that line the inner walls of the blood vessels, providing an opportunity for more fatty deposits to accumulate. This causes the vessels to become more and more constricted as the years go by. Smoke also makes the blood platelets become larger, denser, and stickier. This brings about a thickening of the blood that makes dangerous clotting take place more easily. Regular smoking also lowers the amount of good cholesterol and boosts the bad cholesterol in the blood.

Cigarette smoking is the number-one risk factor of heart disease. It causes fibrillation, raises cholesterol levels in the blood, increases the risk of blood clotting, and starves the cardiac muscles of oxygen.

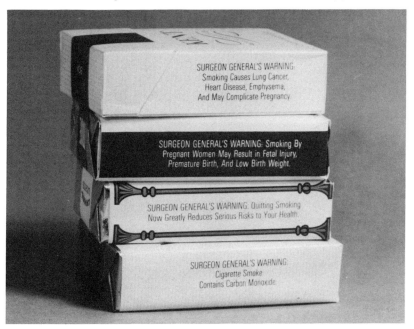

Certainly, some risk factors are out of our control. Cigarette smoking is not one of them. It is the easiest of all the factors to eliminate. Research has shown that one year after a person stops smoking, his or her cholesterol level can return to normal. The risk of having a heart attack for a person who has not smoked for 10 years is the same as that of someone who has never smoked. Quite clearly, a major step in the prevention of heart disease is not smoking.

HIGH BLOOD PRESSURE

High blood pressure, or *hypertension,* is the most common chronic disease in the United States. There are 35 million people who have high blood pressure and another 25 million whose pressure falls within a borderline danger area. Hypertension is believed to play a part in 1,250,000 heart attacks every year.

The heart pumps blood at a certain pressure in order to maintain a supply to all parts of the body. Blood pressure is not the same throughout the body. The pressure is greatest as the blood leaves the heart, and continues to drop until it returns. Not much pressure is lost as blood goes through the trunk and limbs, but pressure drops noticeably in the capillaries and becomes even lower in the veins. When it returns to the heart, blood pressure is less than $1/_{10}$ of what it was at first.

Blood pressure also varies with physical and emotional activity. It rises during exertion and periods of stress and drops to its lowest level during sleep. Pressure-sensitive cells in the large arteries monitor blood pressure and regulate its levels. These cells can send chemical signals to smaller arteries to dilate and contract, as the blood is pumped under more or less pressure.

When blood pressure is measured, the reading on the sphygmomanometer shows the force of blood against the walls of the arteries. This tells the doctor about the condition of the vessels. If the normally elastic arteries are under tension, the blood pressure reading is high. If the arteries are relaxed, the pressure reading is normal.

A normal systolic (contracting) reading is usually between 110 and 140. A diastolic (relaxed) reading of 60 to 90 is considered normal. The two numbers are given together, with systolic pressure over diastolic, as a total reading. People with a reading above 160/95 are considered to have high blood pressure.

Hypertension is often referred to as the "silent killer." This is because there usually are no early symptoms of the disease. The only way to discover its presence is to get a systolic reading at least once a year. Millions of people are totally unaware of their high blood pressure, which if uncontrolled can result in stroke, heart failure, or death.

Hypertension does its greatest damage to the delicate inner lining of the coronary arteries. Under high pressure, blood does not flow smoothly, but crashes along the artery walls much like a rampaging river. If there is a weakness in an artery, the blood under high pressure can rupture the artery. A rupture in an artery to the brain can cause a major stroke, whereas such a rupture in a coronary artery results in a serious heart attack.

Small, patchy deposits of discarded tissue may form at points along the coronary arteries, which are subject to the constant bombardment of rushing blood. These arteries may begin to harden and become blocked. The heart, in turn, receives insufficient oxygen and is required to pump against increased resistance. This condition can lead to coronary artery disease.

There is no single cause of hypertension. About 15% of those with this disease have defects in one of the mechanisms that control blood flow in the body. Some cases are hereditary. In most cases, however, high blood pressure develops because of the habits of the patient. For example, it is three times more prevalent in people who are seriously overweight. According to the Framingham Study, a 15% gain in weight is accompanied by an 18% rise in systolic pressure.

The body needs four grams of salt a day to function properly. Most people take in two to four times this amount every day. The salt (actually, the sodium in the salt) draws additional fluid into the circulatory system and increases the total volume of blood in the body. An increased volume of blood will result in greater blood pressure. Reducing salt intake can reverse this process. With less salt, the total volume of blood decreases. With less fluid in circulation, blood pressure goes down.

Smoking, drinking alcoholic beverages, and stress can also contribute to high blood pressure. Whatever the cause, however, hypertension must be controlled. If treated, high blood pressure can be reduced to normal levels, minimizing the threat of heart attack and sudden death.

Treatment for hypertension varies from patient to patient. In many cases, the doctor will prescribe a change in the habits that have led to an increase in pressure. A person may be told to stop smoking or lose weight. Another may be placed on a low-salt diet or given an exercise regimen to follow. Often, a combination of such changes will bring about a change in pressure.

More serious hypertension patients will be given one or more of the drugs that are now available. The doctor may prescribe a diuretic, which will increase the amount of urine (and therefore, salt) that is excreted. Beta blockers are also used to treat hypertension. These medications can block out the receptors in the heart that speed up the heart rate and increase blood pressure. New calcium blockers help to keep the arteries from hardening and becoming blocked. Other medications can dilate blood vessels that are under higher pressure, act on nerve impulses, or activate special hormones.

The chairman of a national cholesterol education program at a 1987 news conference in Washington, D.C. His panel found that millions of Americans with unacceptably high cholesterol levels are going untreated.

CHOLESTEROL AND HEART DISEASE

For many years, doctors were not sure of the role that cholesterol played in causing heart disease. This controversy ended in 1984 when the National Heart, Lung and Blood Institute released the results of a 10-year study that showed "beyond a shadow of a doubt that for every one percent you lower your blood cholesterol, you lower your chances of having a heart attack by two percent."

Cholesterol is a waxy fatlike substance that is chemically known as a steroid alcohol. It is produced naturally in the body by the liver, and it is needed to build cell membranes, to make certain hormones and digestive bile, and to produce the protective coverings on nerve fibers. Cholesterol does not dissolve in blood plasma; cells wrap it in water-soluble proteins that help it to travel in the bloodstream. These *lipoproteins* become both the good and bad cholesterol compounds in the body.

Low-density lipoproteins (LDL) carry much of the cholesterol in the blood. High levels of this bad cholesterol lead to clogging of the arteries through continuous plaque buildup. High-density lipoproteins (HDL) ferry the cholesterol back to the liver, which digests it. In a way, this good compound helps the body get rid of excess cholesterol. Researchers agree that the balance of good and bad cholesterol, not a total count, is the key to determining the risk of heart disease.

Unfortunately, the human body is capable of producing all the cholesterol it needs. Additional cholesterol enters the body through foods that are popular in the American diet. The American Heart Association recommends that people limit their cholesterol intake to 300 milligrams a day (a bit more than the amount in an egg yolk). Unfortunately, the average American takes in between 400 and 700 milligrams daily. Cholesterol is plentiful in foods that contain saturated fats, which are found mostly in animal products.

Cholesterol levels in the blood can be measured with a simple blood test. Federal guidelines have established a safe cholesterol level for adults: 200 milligrams of cholesterol per $1/_{10}$ liter of blood. More than half of the American adult population have total cholesterol levels that exceed these guidelines. The general rule for cholesterol levels is that a count between 200 and 239 is a signal to restrict the intake of saturated fats. With a count above

239, the blood should be checked to determine the balance between LDL and HDL cholesterol. Normally, a change in diet will lower the cholesterol count. However, in severe cases, especially if there is a history of heart disease and a high LDL reading, diet may not be enough, and it may be necessary to use one of the medications described earlier to lower the cholesterol count.

Changing the way a person eats is the most effective way of lowering LDL levels in the blood. The most important thing is to stay away from saturated fats. This means limiting the intake of luncheon meats, marbled beef, poultry skin, palm and coconut oil, and whole-milk products. Fatty cheeses and dark poultry meats also contain saturated fats. The American Heart Association suggests that fatty foods should not make up more than 30% of a person's daily diet. The key to a healthy diet is to substitute low cholesterol foods for those in which saturated fats are abundant.

Remember that the recommended limit is 300 milligrams of cholesterol a day. Now consider that a whole egg has 250 milligrams and a cup of chicken livers has 746. One cup of 16%-fat ice cream has 84 milligrams of cholesterol, whereas a cup of low-fat yogurt has only 14. A tablespoon of butter has 31 milligrams, but the same amount of margarine has none. Green or yellow vegetables and fruit also have no cholesterol. Obviously, the key to healthy eating is to become aware of the fat and cholesterol content of the foods one eats. In addition, by following a few important rules about preparing foods, it is possible to lower cholesterol intake considerably:

1. Substitute fish and poultry for red meats.
2. Use skim or low-fat milk in place of whole milk.
3. Eat only two or three eggs a week.
4. Limit shrimp and organ meats such as liver to one or two portions a month.
5. Cook with polyunsaturated vegetable oils and margarine.
6. Make sure cooking oil is hot enough before adding food, so that less fat is absorbed.
7. Grill, stew, or stir-fry instead of roasting or deep-frying.
8. Cut down on meat-based gravy. Make gravy after draining off fat.
9. Use no-stick pans that require little or no fat.
10. Use plenty of paper toweling to absorb fats on all foods.

A proper diet is the most effective way to lower cholesterol levels in the blood. Green or yellow vegetables and fruits are cholesterol-free.

To be sure, food is not the only factor involved in determining cholesterol levels. It has already been mentioned that cigarette smoking raises LDL levels and lowers beneficial HDL levels. Studies show that some aerobic exercises increase good cholesterol in the blood and that stress alters the balance for the worse. Still, diet is unquestionably the most important means of controlling cholesterol levels.

STRESS AND EXERCISE

Life is filled with stress—at home, on the job, and in between. Stress is emotional pressure, the wrong sort of pressure. It is a reaction to the changes that people are forced to encounter every day of their life. The greater the change, the greater the stress. And as studies show, the greater the stress, the greater the risk of heart attack.

One study entitled "The Social Readjustment Scale," published in the *Journal of Psychosomatic Research* in 1967 by Dr. T. Holmes and Dr. R. Rahe of the Naval Neuropsychiatric Unit in San Diego, California, showed that heart attacks were often preceded by an abrupt change in the person's life three to six months before the attack. The study also demonstrated that the greater the change, the shorter the time before the onset of the attack. It also revealed a correlation between the most abrupt changes and the most severe heart attacks.

Researchers have found that some people learn how to deal effectively with stress. Others not only fail to cope with external stress but create their own stress as well. Several decades ago, two cardiologists, Dr. Ray Rosenmann and Dr. Meyer Friedman, both of the Harold Brunn Institute of Mount Zion Hospital in San Francisco, described Type-A and Type-B personalities. Type-A are competitive, driven, and aggressive people who do everything in a hurry. In contrast, Type-B people are easygoing and relaxed. They do not hurry to do anything and are not interested in competing with co-workers or neighbors. Type-A people have been found to be coronary prone. Their rate of heart attacks is very high compared to those of Type-B people. Type-A people tend to be easily irritated; find it difficult to relax; are impatient; take on more work than they can handle; get very upset when things do not go their way; have difficulty solving problems at home; eat too quickly; and talk and gesture excessively. Learning to deal with stress involves making changes in the way one lives. Type-A people must recognize their limitations and learn to say no to demands that are too much for them. Most important, they must find a balance between rest and activity and seek healthy outlets, such as sports and exercise, that will help them place stressful situations in their proper perspective.

Some experts have found that relaxation can act as a buffer between stress and unhealthy reactions in the body. For example, Dr. Herbert Benson of the Harvard Medical School uses transcendental meditation to lower blood-pressure levels in his patients. Transcendental meditation involves the chanting of a "mantra"—a word or a sound spoken repeatedly to help focus the mind and enter a meditative state. Biofeedback is another relaxation technique. During biofeedback a visual display of heart rate, blood pressure, and other body functions are fed back to the person, who then tries to exert mental influence over a particular function in ordeer to control it.

Many people use water (hydrotherapy) in a sauna, Jacuzzi, or hot tub as a form of relaxation. Other people find a regular time each day to do something relaxing, such as listening to music or pursuing a hobby. A special time away from stress sometimes fortifies people with the ability to face the pressures that are to follow. If abrupt change can bring on a heart attack, perhaps learning to take the edge off, and learning to respond to change, can help the body to survive each new crisis as it comes.

In recent years, researchers have become very interested in how exercise influences heart disease. In 1987, Carl J. Caspersen and Kenneth Powell of the Centers for Disease Control concluded that physical inactivity is the most common threat of all. Their analysis of 43 other studies showed that people who are inactive face twice the risk of having a heart attack, about the same risk as people who smoke heavily, have high blood pressure, or have high cholesterol.

Another study, entitled "Work Energy Level: Personal Characteristics and Fatal Heart Attacks," published in the *American Journal of Epidemiology* in 1977 by Dr. Ralph S. Paffenbarger, MD., of Stanford University, examined over 12,000 men in high-risk categories, and he concluded that those men who regularly did home repairs, went dancing, or had other moderate activity, had 40% fewer heart attacks than men who were less active.

Regular exercise can reduce the stress that leads to heart attack. A 1987 study showed that people who are inactive face twice the risk of having a heart attack as do people who engage in regular, moderate exercise.

Researchers feel that heart muscles get stronger, and HDL levels rise, during moderate physical activity. For the millions of people who do no exercise at all, experts at the Centers for Disease Control recommend a half-hour walk every day as a first step to better health.

High blood pressure also seems to respond to exercise therapy. In a study done in Melbourne, Australia, 13 people with mild hypertension rode exercise bicycles for 40 minutes, 3 times a week. After several months of this regular exercise, the blood pressure of many of the subjects was down to normal. For these men and women, exercise was as effective as any antihypertensive drug.

The heart is a remarkable organ. It serves us faithfully, 24 hours a day, for a lifetime. Understanding the heart, its blood vessels, and the blood it pumps to our trillions of cells, may make that lifetime healthier, longer, and more fruitful.

•　　　•　　　•　　　•

APPENDIX:
FOR MORE INFORMATION

The following is a list of associations and organizations that can provide further information on the circulatory system and circulatory and blood disorders. Divisions of the National Institutes of Health and the American Heart Association can refer you to treatment centers and medical specialists in your area.

American Cancer Society
90 Park Avenue
New York, NY 10016
212-599-8200

American Heart Association
7320 Greenville Avenue
Dallas, TX 75231
214-373-6300

Association of Heart Patients
P.O. Box 54305
Atlanta, GA 30308
800-241-6993
404-523-0826

Cooley's Anemia Foundation
105 East 22nd Street, Suite 911
New York, NY 10010
212-598-0911

The Coronary Club, Inc.
Cleveland Clinical Educational
  Foundation
9500 Euclid Avenue
Cleveland, OH 44106

Division of Blood Diseases and
  Resources
National Heart, Lung, and Blood
  Institute
Bethesda, MD 20892

High Blood Pressure Information
  Center
120/80 National Institutes of Health
Bethesda, MD 20892
301-496-1809

International Association for Heart
  Transplantation
435 North Michigan Avenue
Suite 177
Chicago, IL 60611
312-644-0828

National Heart, Lung, and Blood
  Institute
National Institutes of Health
Building 31
Room 4A21
Bethesda, MD 20892
301-496-4236

National Hemophilia Foundation
19 West 34th Street
New York, NY 10001

National Institute of Neurological
and Communicative Disorders
and Stroke
National Institutes of Health
Bethesda, MD 20892

World Federation of Hemophilia
Suite 2902
1155 Dorchester Boulevard,W.
Montreal, Quebec H3B 2L3

FURTHER READING

The American Heart Association. *Heart Book: A Guide to Prevention and Treatment of Cardiovascular Diseases.* New York: Dutton, 1980.

American Medical Association. *Guide to Heart Care.* New York: Random House, 1984.

Amsterdam, Ezra A. *Take Care of Your Heart.* New York: Facts on File, 1984.

Barnard, Christiaan, M.D., and Peter Evans. *Your Healthy Heart.* New York: McGraw-Hill, 1985.

Comroe, Julius H., Jr., M.D. *Exploring the Heart: Discoveries in Heart Disease and High Blood Pressure.* New York: Norton, 1983.

Davis, Goode P. *The Heart: The Living Pump.* Washington, DC: U.S. News Books, 1981.

DeBakey, Michael. *The Living Heart Diet.* New York: Raven Press/Simon and Schuster, 1984.

Drotar, David Lee. *Micro-Surgery: Revolution in the Operating Room.* New York: Beaufort Books, 1981.

Elgin, Kathleen. *The Heart.* New York: Franklin Watts, 1968.

Farndon, John. *The All Color Book of the Body.* New York: Arco, 1985.

Friedman, Meyer, M.D., and Diane Ulmer, R.N. *Treating Type A Behavior and Your Heart.* New York: Knopf, 1984.

Hoffman, Nancy Yanes. *The Bypass Experience.* New York: Harcourt Brace Jovanovich, 1985.

Lavin, John H. *Stroke: From Crisis to Victory: A Family Guide.* New York: Franklin Watts, 1985.

Leinwald, Gerald. *Transplants: Today's Medical Miracles.* New York: Franklin Watts, 1985.

Poole, Victoria. *Thursday's Child*. Boston: Little, Brown, 1980.

Smith, Anthony. *The Body*. New York: Viking, 1986.

Tigen, Steven. *Heart Disease*. New York: Julian Messner, 1986.

U.S. Department of Health and Human Services, Public Health Service, National Institutes of Health. *The Fourteenth Report of the National Heart, Lung, and Blood Advisory Council*. NIH Publication No. 87-2729. Bethesda, MD: 1987.

Whitaker, Julian. *Reversing Heart Disease*. New York: Warner Books, 1985.

Zim, Herbert S. *Your Heart and How It Works*. New York: William Morrow, 1959.

GLOSSARY

adventitia the outside layer of an artery or vein; composed of strong fibers and connective tissue

albumin a protein, one form of which is carried by blood plasma, that can prevent hemorrhaging

anemia blood disorder due to a lack of circulating red blood cells or hemoglobin, or a depleted total volume of blood

aneurism ballooning in the wall of the heart or of a blood vessel

angina pectoris a disease marked by severe chest pain and constriction

antibody a protein produced by the body to combat bacteria, viruses, or other foreign substances

anticoagulant a drug that interferes with and sometimes prevents clotting

aorta the largest artery in the body

arrhythmia a disruption in the heart's natural rhythm

artery a blood vessel that carries blood away from the heart

arteriosclerosis a hardening, thickening, and loss of elasticity of the artery walls

atherosclerosis the process of plaque buildup and degeneration of the arterial lining

atrium either section of the upper area of the heart, which is divided into left and right chambers

beta blockers drugs used to treat angina and hypertension

biptome device used to monitor the body's acceptance or rejection of a heart transplant

bypass surgery operation to bypass a blocked artery

capillary a microscopic, linking blood vessel

cardiopulmonary resuscitation (CPR) a procedure designed to restore normal breathing after cardiac arrest; includes the clearance of air passages to the lungs, heart massage, and the administration of therapeutic drugs

catheter a thin tube that can be inserted into the body for draining or injecting fluids

channel blocker a drug that prevents arterial spasms

cholesterol a waxy, fatlike substance produced in the liver or ingested in the form of saturated fats

clot a thick, jellylike mass produced by platelets

coagulate to clot

coarctation a congenital narrowing of the blood vessels; results in a slowing of the blood flow and possible heart failure

congenital present from birth

coronary circulation the local route of blood to and from the heart by which the heart receives its own supply of oxygen and nutrients

corpuscle any cell or small mass not connected to form continuous tissue, e.g., a blood cell

diastole the relaxation stage of the heart muscle in its normal cyclical rhythm

digitalis heart medicine made from the foxglove plant

diuretic a substance that increases salt and water excretion from the kidney, increasing production of urine

electrocardiograph (EKG) a machine that detects and charts the size and direction of a heart muscle's contractions through electric currents sent through the heart muscle

embolism the obstruction of a blood vessel caused by a clot or other mass

embolus a blood clot or other mass that detaches from the vessel wall and circulates throughout the blood system, causing obstruction at another point

endarterectomy surgical removal of plaque (done by opening an artery and scraping away at its walls with a blunt instrument) or of the portion of a vessel's inner wall containing a clot or obstruction

endocardium the layer of cells that line the heart walls

erythrocytes red blood cells

fibrillation uncoordinated contractions of the heart's muscles

fibrin a fibrous, clot-forming material in the blood

fibrinogen a protein secreted by the liver into the plasma that, when converted to fibrin, is essential in clotting

gamma globulin any of a class of proteins found in plasma, many of which act as antibodies

hemoglobin an iron compound found in red blood cells that carries oxygen from the lungs to the body's tissues

hemophilia a hereditary disease characterized by delayed clotting of blood, which can lead to hemorrhaging even after minor injuries

hyperemia tissue congestion caused by blockage of blood and resulting in possible tissue destruction

hypertension high blood pressure

insulin a digestive hormone produced by the pancreas, essential for proper processing of blood sugar and for maintenance of the proper blood-sugar level

Jarvik-7 a mechanical or artificial heart, designed by the U.S. cardiologist Robert Jarvik

laser angioplasty the use of laser beams through a tipped catheter to remove plaque in a clogged artery

leukemia any of a group of acute blood diseases characterized by an unrestrained growth of leukocytes

leukocyte a white blood cell

lovastatin a drug that reduces cholesterol levels

lymph system an independent circulation system for lymphocytes in the body

lymphocyte a variety of white blood cell involved in immunity; includes B-lymphocytes and T-lymphocytes

mitral valve a valve that prevents blood from flowing backward in the heart; located between the left atrium and left ventricle

monocyte a white blood cell whose function is to ingest germs, bacteria, and foreign particles

nitroglycerine a chemical that can open clogged blood vessels

nutrients substances in food essential to metabolism

pacemaker a device implanted into the chest to set the heart's rhythm

pericardium sacs surrounding and covering the heart

phagocytes white blood cells that engulf and destroy germs, bacteria, and small particles

plaque a localized abnormal part on a body surface, such as an artery wall

plasma the liquid part of blood

platelets blood cells that control clotting

pulmonary circulation the route of blood to and from the lungs

rhesus (Rh) factor an important protein in the blood capable of inducing allergic reactions

secretin a digestive hormone found in plasma

septum a wall separating two cavities, especially the left and right sides of the heart

sinoatrial node the heart's own pacemaker, located in the upper region of the right atrium

sphygmomanometer a mercury pressure gauge used to measure blood pressure

systemic circulation the route of blood to and from body parts

systole the normal, rythmic contraction of heart muscles

thrombin a chemical released by platelets that converts fibrinogen into fibrin, helping to form clots

thrombophlebitis blockage and consequential inflammation of a vein

thrombosis forming of blood clots in blood vessels in the coronary artery

thrombus a plug or clot inside living tissue, attached to the wall of a blood vessel

thyroxin a hormone found in plasma and used in the treatment of hypothyroidism

tricuspid valve a valve composed of three flaps, or cusps, which is located between the right atrium and the right ventricle

ultrasound echocardiography a diagnostic procedure using high frequency sound waves to diagnose heart problems

vein a blood vessel that carries blood from the body back to the heart

vena cava either of two large veins—superior or inferior—by which blood is returned to the right atrium of the heart

ventricle either of the two lower, pumping chambers of the heart

INDEX

Abdomen, 19
Acidophiles, 50
Acquired Heart Disease, 64–66, 82
   symptoms of, 64–65
Acute indigestion, 66
Adrenaline, 45
Adventitia, 39
Agote, Luis, 26
AIDS (acquired immune deficiency
      syndrome), 55
Albumin, 46
Alcoholic beverages, 89
American diet, 91
American Heart Association, 14, 91,
   92
American Journal of Epidemiology,
   95
Amino acids, 45
Amoebas, 49
Anatomy, 19
Anemia, 15, 57–58
   hemolytic, 57–58
   pernicious, 57
   sickle-cell, 58
Aneurysm, 69, 83
Angina pectoris, 65
Angiograms, 76
Animal transfusions, 22–23
Antibiotics, 62
Antibodies, 45, 50–51, 54
Anticoagulants, 80
Antitoxins, 24
Aorta, 39, 42, 61–62
Aortic valves, 83
Apex, 32

Aquapendente, Fabricius de, 20, 21
Arrhythmia, 81
Arteries, 20, 22, 28, 36–40, 42, 61,
   65, 73, 77, 88, 89
Arterioles, 36, 42
Arthritis, 62
Artificial heart, 30
Artificial valves, 83
Aspirin, 81
Atherosclerosis, 66
Atria, 30, 31, 33–34, 35, 41, 42, 60
Atrial septum defects, 60
Autoimmune response, 62
Azathioprine, 84

Baby Fae, 84
Bacteria, 25, 51
Bacterial fragment, 63
Balloon angioplasty, 77
Balloon pump, 77
Barnard, Christiaan, 29, 83
Base, 32
Basophils, 50
Battery pack, 79
Baylor College Medical Center, 82
Beats. *See* Heartbeats
Behring, Emil von, 25
Benson, Herbert, 94
Beta blockers, 80, 90
Bigelow, Wilfred, 28–29
Biofeedback, 94
Biological valves, 83
Biotome, 84
Blaiberg, Philip, 29
Blalock, John, 27–28

Blood, 16
circulation of, 22, 32, 33–34
disorders of, 15, 55–58
donation of, 55
flow, 15, 18, 20, 23–34, 34, 36, 43
leakage of, 27
oxygen-poor, 27
parts of, 15, 43–52
pumped, 34, 35, 36–40, 41–42
route of, 20–21
as sustainer of life, 17–19
types of, 25, 52–55
whole, 44–45
Blood banks, 55
Bloodletting, 17, 22
Blood pressure, 23, 73, 87, 88–90, 94, 95, 96
Blood pressure cuff, 25, 73
Blood tissue, 44
Blood transfusions, 22–23
Blood vessels, 14, 16, 18, 22, 26, 31, 36–40, 44, 46, 52, 66, 69, 73, 76, 81
blocked, 28
Blood-vessel surgery, 29
Blue baby, 27
Blundell, James, 24–25
Bone marrow, 48–49, 58
Brain cells, 44
Breastbone, 32, 67
Bundle of His, 35
Bypass procedure, 22, 83

Calcium, 66
Capillaries, 40, 42, 47
Carbon dioxide, 31
removal of, 31, 47
Carbon monoxide, 87
Cardiac arrest, 69–70
Cardiac catheter, 75–76
Cardiac catheterization, 26
Cardiac glycosides, 79
Cardiac muscle, 26, 32, 74
Cardiologist, 71, 74, 75
Cardiovascular disease, 15, 16, 86
causes of, 14–16
Carotid bypass, 29
Caspersen, Carl J., 95

Catheter, 26, 80
Centers for Disease Control, 93, 96
Chambers, 14, 34, 35, 76
Channel blockers, 80
Chest cavity, 32
Chest compression, 67, 70
Cholesterol, 16, 66, 81, 85
and heart disease, 91–93, 95
Cigarette smoking, 60, 86–88
and heart disease, 86–88
Circulatory shock, 46
Circulatory system, 18
damage done by cigarette smoking, 87
disorders of, 59
functions of, 32
parts of, 32
path of, 41–42
problems related to, 15, 16, 73, 86–88, 91–93
Clark, Barney, 30
Clots, 26, 51–52, 55–57, 66, 80, 83, 87
Coarctation, 61
Cohn, Edwin J., 46–47
Colombo, Realdo, 20
Congenital heart defects, 15, 60–62
Congestive heart failure, 69
Constrictive pericarditis, 64
Contraction, 35, 42
Coronary artery, 52, 65, 68–69, 77
Coronary Artery Disease (CAD), 14, 16, 65, 66, 73, 86, 89
Coronary bypass, 82
Coronary thrombosis, 55, 68
corpuscles, 52, 57
CPR (cardio-pulmonary resuscitation), 67, 70
Cutler, E., 26
Cyclosporine, 84

Damaged valves, 23
De Bakey, Michael, 82
Denis, Jean-Baptiste, 22
De Vries, William, 30
Diastole, 36
Diastolic reading, 88–89
Dicumarol, 55

Digestive organs, 39
Diuretics, 81
Division of Artificial Organs, 30
Drugs, 60
Ductus arteriosus, 61, 63
Dynamite, 80

Einthoven, Willem, 26
Electrocardiograph (EKG), 26, 73–75
  ambulatory, 75
  stress, 75
Embolism, 56
Embolus, 56
Endarterectomy, 83
Endocarditis, 63
Endocardium, 33
Erasistratus, 18
Examination, 72–73
Exercise, 93–96

Fat cells, 49
Fat digestion, 49
Fatty acids, 45
Fatty deposits, 78, 87
Fibrillation, 69–70, 74, 86
Fibrin, 52, 56
Fibrinogen, 52
Fibrous bone tissue, 66
Forssmann, Werner, 26
Framingham Heart Study, 85–86, 89
Friedman, Meyer, 94

Galen, 18–20
Gamma globulin, 46
Garrett, Edward, 82
Gemfibrozil, 81
German measles, 60
Germs, 25, 50, 51
Gibbon, John, 29
Globulins, 45
Glucose, 45
Glycogen, 45
Gross, Robert, 27

Hales, Stephen, 23
Harold Brunn Institute of Mount
    Sinai Hospital, 94
Harvard Medical School, 27

Harvard University, 46, 81
Harvey, William, 19–22, 29
Heart, 14, 16, 31–32
  functions of, 31–32, 34–36, 41–42
  history of study of, 17–30
  parts of, 32–34
  problems with, 59–70
  prevention of, 85–96
  treatment of, 71–84
Heart attack, 14, 52, 55, 66–69, 86–
    87
Heartbeat, 14, 34, 35, 36
Heart defects, 60
Heart disease, 15, 16, 59, 85–86
Heart medications, 79
Heart muscle, 15
Heart surgery, 29, 82–83
Heart transplant, 16, 83–84
Hemoglobin, 47, 49
Hemophilia, 15, 56
Hemorrhaging, 25
Hennekens, Charles H., 81
Hepatitis, 47
High blood pressure, 15, 73, 88–90
High-density lipoproteins (HDL), 91,
    92, 96
His, Vilhelm, 35
Holmes, T., 93
Hormones, 45, 90
Houttar, Henry, 26
Hydrotherapy, 94
Hyperemia, 55
Hypertension. See High blood pres-
    sure

Immune system, 63
Infarction, 68
Infection, 50
Infectious bacteria, 62
Infectious diseases, 62–64
Infective endocarditis, 63
Inferior venae cavae, 40, 42
Insulin, 45
Intima, 36
Iron, 49
Isotope, 76

Jacobson, Julius, 29

Jarvik, Robert, 30
Jarvik-7 artificial heart, 30
Johns Hopkins University, 27
Journal of Psychosomatic Research,
     93

Kantorowicz, Adrian, 29
Kidneys, 46

Laennec, Rene T. H., 24
Landsteiner, Karl, 25–26
Laser angioplasty, 78
Lasers, 77–78
Leeuwenhoek, Antoni van, 22
Left ventricle, 34, 39, 42, 61
Leukemia, 15
Leukocytes, 49–51
Levine, S. A., 26
Lipoprotein, 81, 91
   high density, 91, 93, 96
   low density, 91, 93
Liver, 45
Louis XIV (king of France), 22
Lung artery. *See* Pulmonary artery
Lymph glands, 50
Lymph nodes, 50, 51
Lymphocytes, 50

Malpighi, Marcello, 22
Marrow, 49
Media, 36
Metchnikoff, Elie, 25
Microscope, 22
Microsurgery, 29–30
Minerals, 45
Mitral valve, 34, 63, 83
Monocytes, 50
Moulin, Allen, 22–23
Muscle cells, 44
Myocardial infarction, 68
Myocarditis, 63

National Bone Marrow Registry, 58
National Heart, Lung and Blood In-
     stitute, 91
Naval Neuropsychiatric Unit, 93
Nerve cells, 44
Neutrophils, 50

New England Journal of Medicine,
   The, 81
Nicoumalone, 80
Nitrates, 80
Nitrites, 80
Nitroglycerine, 80
Nobel Prize, 26
Nutrients, 45

One-way valves, 21
On the Movement of the Heart and
     Blood in Animals (Harvey),
     21
Open-heart surgery, 28–29, 76
Oxygen, 27, 40, 42
   circulation of, 41–42

Pacemaker, 29, 79
Paffenbarger, Ralph S., 95
Pancreas, 49
Patent ductus arteriosus, 61
Penicillin, 63
Pericardial effusion, 64
Pericarditis, 63–64
Pericardium, 33
Plaque, 66, 80
Plasma, 44, 45–47
Platelets, 15, 44–45, 51–52, 56
Powell, Kenneth, 95
Propranolol, 80
Proteins, 45
Protozoa, 49
Pulmonary artery, 39, 41, 61
Pulmonary circulation, 41
Pulmonary veins, 41
Pulse, 39

Radioisotopes, 76
Rahe, R., 93
Red blood cells, 44–45, 47–49, 54,
     57–58
Red Cross, 67
Rehn, Ludwig, 25
Rhesus factor, 54
Rheumatic fever, 63
Right ventricle, 34, 41
Rosenbaum, Ray, 94
Royal College of Physicians, 20

Salt, 89
Saturated fats, 91
Scar-tissue cells, 51
Science Digest, 14
Secretin, 45
Septum, 34, 35
Septum defects, 60
Sinoatrial node, 34–35
Sinus node. See Sinoatrial node
Skin, 39
Skin cells, 44
"Social Readjustment Scale, The," 93
Sodium, 89
Sphygmomanometer, 73
Spleen, 49
Steroids, 84
Stethoscope, 24, 72
Stomach, 49
Stress, 93–95
Stroke, 89
Superior venae cavae, 41
Systemic route, 41
Systole, 36

Thrombin, 52
Thrombophlebitis, 55
Thrombosis, 55, 68
Thrombus, 52, 55
Thyroxin, 45
Tissue plasminogen activator (t-PA), 80–81
Transcendental meditation, 94
Tricuspid valve, 34, 41

Tuffier, 25
Type-A personalities, 94
Type-B personalities, 94

Ultrasound echocardiograph, 76
Universal donor, 53
Universal recipient, 53
University of Padua, 19, 20
University of Utah College of Medicine, 30
University of Vermont Medical School, 29

Valves, 14, 40, 76
Veins, 36, 39, 40, 41, 42, 47
Ventricle, 33–34, 78
Ventricular septal defect, 60
Venules, 36, 41, 42
Vesalius, Andreas, 19–20
Vitamins, 45
Voluntary muscle, 32

Warfarin, 80
Washansky, Louis, 29
White blood cells, 15, 44–45, 49–51, 58
"Work Energy Level: Personal Characteristics and Fatal Heart Attacks" (Paffenbarger), 95

X ray, 26–27, 73, 76

"Your Heart: A Survival Guide," 14

PICTURE CREDITS

AP/Wide World Photos: pp. 28, 71, 74, 77, 82, 86, 90; The Bettmann Archive: pp. 18, 23; Culver Pictures, Inc.: pp. 17, 19, 20, 24; Debra P. Hershkowitz: p. 85; National Heart, Lung, and Blood Institute: pp. 54, 56; National Library of Medicine: p. 27; Taurus Photos: pp. 13, 14, 31, 40, 43, 44, 53, 57, 59, 62, 65, 67, 68, 72, 78, 87, 93, 95; Original illustrations by Robert Margulies: pp. 33, 37, 38, 48, 61

Regina Avraham has been a science teacher with the New York City Board of Education since the 1960s. She also edits and writes textbooks and general-interest books for young adults. She is the author of *The Downside of Drugs* in the Chelsea HOUSE ENCYCLOPEDIA OF PSYCHOACTIVE DRUGS, series 2. Ms. Avraham currently teaches biology and coordinates a science magnet program in New York City.

Dale C. Garell, M.D., is medical director of California Childrens Services, Department of Health Services, County of Los Angeles. He is also clinical professor in the Department of Pediatrics and Family Medicine at the University of Southern California School of Medicine and Visiting associate clinical professor of maternal and child health at the University of Hawaii School of Public Health. From 1963 to 1974, he was medical director of the Division of Adolescent Medicine at Children's Hospital in Los Angeles. Dr. Garell has served as president of the Society for Adolescent Medicine, chairman of the youth committee of the American Academy of Pediatrics, and as a forum member of the White House Conference on Children (1970) and White House Conference on Youth (1971). He has also been a member of the editorial board of the *American Journal of Diseases of Children.*

C. Everett Koop, M.D., Sc.D., is Surgeon General, Deputy Assistant Secretary for Health, and Director of the Office of International Health of the U.S. Public Health Service. A pediatric surgeon with an international reputation, he was previously surgeon-in-chief of Children's Hospital of Philadelphia and professor of pediatric surgery and pediatrics at the University of Pennsylvania. Dr. Koop is the author of more than 175 articles and books on the practice of medicine. He has served as surgery editor of the *Journal of Clinical Pediatrics* and editor-in-chief of the *Journal of Pediatric Surgery.* Dr. Koop has received nine honorary degrees and numerous other awards, including the Denis Brown Gold Medal of the British Association of Paediatric Surgeons, the William E. Ladd Gold Medal of the American Academy of Pediatrics, and the Copernicus Medal of the Surgical Society of Poland. He is a Chevalier of the French Legion of Honor and a member of the Royal College of Surgeons, London.